GOOD PLANETS ARE HARD TO BUY

A Management Handbook for Creating Conscious Capitalism, Sustainability Principles and Supply Chain Excellence

LARRY BERGLUND

Good Planets Are Hard To Buy

Copyright © 2016 Larry Berglund

Buddha Press

ISBN: 978-1-517450-9-53

Cover Art by Graeme Berglund
Cover design by Ares Jun

For Nancy

And our grandchildren and their planet.

TABLE OF CONTENTS

Introduction

When all the trees have been cut down,
when all the animals have been hunted,
when all the waters are polluted,
when all the air is unsafe to breathe,
only then will you discover you cannot eat money.
~ Cree Prophecy

Good news: we live on a beautiful and bountiful planet. Bad news: as far as we can see in all directions, we are the one and only spinning orb of life. In other words, this is it! You would think therefore, that we creatures with the big brains who make the biggest impact on it would get it through our collective craniums that we need to take extra special care of this planet.

We have been in the position of exploiting people, extorting riches and consuming resources without paying the full cost for doing so. The attitude of *live for today because there may not be a tomorrow* has resulted in a self-fulfilling prophecy as there soon won't be enough left for the generations that follow who will be living in our tomorrow. As per the United Nations Environment Programme, $50 billion dollars of food is thrown away each year! We who enjoyed the meal are not the ones who will have to foot the bill, but are putting it on credit for someone else (our children and grandchildren) to discharge the debt. Not a very honorable legacy. The good news—this is starting to change.

As a supply management professional and consultant, I say that caring for our planetary home doesn't have to be at the cost of that other thing that we creatures with the big frontal cortexes are good at: running successful, profitable businesses.

I'm a strong believer that it will be through technology—where creative ideas abound—that we will find long-term solutions to the barrage of problems that continue to have a negative and cumulative effect on our planet. I believe that it can be through the ingenuity of entrepreneurs and the driving force of business, rather than simply through reactive regulations, that positive changes to the environment and society will eventually have a more beneficent effect on a global scale.

My intention with this book is to look at both practical and progressive ways sustainability strategies can be put into practice in any corporation… starting today! I will draw upon my many years of experience as well as the interviews I conducted with many experts in a variety of fields as well as respond to the comments of disbelievers, deniers, and serendipitous dreamers. My preference is to make a difference where I can and share what does and does not work. Perfect solutions rarely exist. The intent is to expand the awareness on issues that we can influence and contribute to more responsible business practices.

I use the terms sustainability and Corporate Social Responsibility (CSR), synonymously throughout the book. In general, the public sector uses the term sustainability while the private sector sees corporate social responsibility as their point of reference. The ideas in this book are based upon continuously trying to understand and learn about the effects embedded in corporate socially responsible and sustainable business practices. My focus is on linking corporate leadership and supply management issues to this controversial subject matter.

Just a few short years ago sustainability or corporate social responsibility was something that organizations whispered about, capitalists feared, activists demanded, and only a few leaders took on with passion and zeal. But CSR is not a form of socialism. CSR is not incompatible with capitalist ideologies. CSR does not mean we have to lose market share. CSR does not mean a loss of profits. CSR is not just for big organizations. CSR is not a fad. CSR does not replace government responsibilities. CSR is not a marketing campaign. CSR is not an oxymoron. Quite simply, CSR is a means of sharing the wealth and being responsible for the resources which are deployed to contribute to the well-being of all.

Sustainability goes far beyond going green. A full implementation of corporate social responsibility requires us to rethink our current strategies in order to extract resources in a less harmful way. CSR requires us to consider these crucial responsibilities in our businesses:

- To use local food sources and indigenous materials to complement imported goods rather than outsourcing their supply
- To substantially reduce the tons of waste going into landfills
- To reduce harmful emissions into the air
- To reduce effluent discharge into waterways
- To treat all peoples with a dignity and not exploit their weaknesses
- To harvest all renewable resources (such as fish and lumber stocks) in a manner that will continue to regenerate a sustainable level for future needs
- To examine our over-use of products to solve issues instead of promoting direct preventative solutions (i.e. pharmaceuticals as a means of addressing health issues)

- To evaluate how increasing crop yield by adding chemicals may eventually lead to the demise of critical nutrients.
- To create profitable enterprises with integrity
- To insist on responsible leadership
- To practice conscious capitalism

I will be touching on all of the above points through examples and stories, both positive and negative, with an aim to inspire, caution and provide practical approaches that you can put into practice. In addition, I have gathered information from a variety of relevant sources and assembled them into manageable and easy-to-understand ideas with clear implementation guidelines that you can take to your management, business and corporate leaders.

Why, Who, How... *plus*

Like any good journalist, I've looked at the kind of questions a skeptic in the business sector might offer when confronted with the term *Corporate Social Responsibility*. I've put both the questions and my research that provides you with informed responses to intelligently address the imperatives of CSR in today's business world. They are set out in: *Why, Who* and *How* sections in this book. We have also added the *Where to Focus First* to help guide you in making the greatest impact in the shortest amount of time, and *How Are We Doing* section to tell you what to do after implementation and give you some benchmarks and some cautions.

The *Why* Section includes a selection of best arguments to take to Chief Officers and entrepreneurs or to share with others in the supply chain field. It also includes *Why Now*—a section that underscores the urgency that faces us now. *Why Now* examines competitive reasons, as well as the obvious social reasons of why organizations should actively be adopting these ideals as soon as possible.

The *Who* section gives a brief overview of the critical organizations and stakeholders that are required to make this a global success, and the roles they need to play in the business sphere. These include Supply Chain Managers, Entrepreneurs, Non-Governmental Organizations (NGOs), Third-party Auditors, Philanthropic Organizations, and the Consumers themselves.

Just how all of these factions are going to achieve the sustainability required to ensure both the planet's and their own survival is addressed in the final three sections of this book entitled, *How, Where to Focus First* and *How Are We Doing*. Along with great suggestions and organizational tools I have included stories and examples from organizations who are doing it right, as well as cautionary tales of those who are giving all enterprise a bad name. Some reputations will be trashed when compared with the organizations people will want to support. Corporations who do not get on board by embracing CSR are undermining their own future well-being, as well as that of future generations.

We are entrenched in a culture where we believe we can buy our way out of anything in a pinch, but that mentality is about to change drastically as we come to terms with the fact that *Good Planets are* not just *Hard to Buy* they are impossible to replace. My wish is that this book gives managers and business people of all kinds the inspiration, courage, wisdom and ammunition to fight for doing the right thing, as well as the tools to do it.

- Larry Berglund

Why?

Why?

A man is ethical only when life, as such, is sacred to him,
that of plants and animals as that of his fellow men
and when he devotes himself helpfully to all life that is in need of his help.
~ Albert Schweitzer

It may seem obvious as to why we should invest in sustainability rather than pursuing our present disastrous environmental and social course. But shockingly, those who hold the power of making the necessary changes have not grasped all the arguments in favor of sustainability. And, among the arguments that have gotten through, many people remain unconvinced. There is an underlying apathy or inertia that makes it difficult to influence affirmative change.

There are those who contend that real change will not happen until the situation reaches crisis level. And others who say we have already reached that level but that the need for change remains invisible in its day-to-day impact.

The only option is to persist in bringing forward arguments that appeal to those in business, and to treat business people as human beings who wish to do the right thing. In short, many of the arguments need to touch on both business and humanitarian issues. However, the problem seems to be that we have left doing the "right thing" to our leaders, at the same time that there has been a loss of integrity in business world. This would come under the heading of being ethical.

What is Ethical?

There have been so many devastating examples in the past decade of how a stunning lack of ethics motivated by greed has lead to tragic and widespread consequences that it is almost easier to speak about what is *not* ethical, rather than what is ethical in how we have been doing business on this planet.

Ethics is an imposed standard of moral principles of right and wrong conduct. It can be debated and often is in the areas we call gray or unclear, and even in areas that seem clear but simply have different agendas or belief systems motivating them. However, in many ethics, the simpler and irrefutable concepts comes from what is best for the whole, meaning the greatest number of people, regardless of their origins, for the longest amount of time. At this point in our history, when it comes to arguing ethics for the whole, and arguing for sustainability we are including the whole planet, not just human beings.

From this perspective, I want to remind everyone of this pivotal albeit negative human trait, greed, and how it has shaped us in recent decades and shaped the world we find ourselves in.

The Greed Factor

In 2002, *Enron* led the pack as the epitome of illegal escapades by large corporations. *Enron's* leaders invented, encouraged and allowed criminal and unethical behaviors under the rationale of increasing share value to their investors. It wasn't the first time that this excuse was used, and unfortunately it won't be the last. It was, however, certainly one of the most damaging and ironically in the long run devastated the shareholder's value, caused audacious personal financial ruin and despair as employees were laid off without the pensions they had paid into, and contributed to the near-bankruptcy of the normally wealthy state of California.

Due to the *Enron* fiasco, the SOX Act (named after Senators Sarbanes and Oxley) introduced standards for corporate fiscal accountability, compliance and whistleblower protection. SOX may keep honest people honest, but it still doesn't curb the behaviour of people bent on putting greed before morals. Only a short six years later in September 2008, the Wall Street meltdown was wholly motivated by the same kind of greed and disregard for ethics. Money lenders encouraged people to sign off on mortgages that lacked fiscal due diligence and like a pyramid scheme it all came tumbling down when interest rates on the re-mortgaging became unsustainable for thousands of people. And yet, *Lehman Brothers* had a $2 billion dollar bonus fund set aside to reward its executives. Lehman CEO, Dick Fuld, was paid $22 million in a 2007 pay packet. Former *Merrill Lynch* CEO, Stan O'Neil, left with a $161 million payout. *Merrill Lynch* lost $8 billion that year and was finally rescued by the *Bank of America* in 2008. In 2007, Bear *Stearns* CEO, James Cayne, received $33.6 million before *Bear Stearns* collapsed.

It is estimated that CEO pay is more than 400 times the average worker's pay in North American business. The large bailout by the US government of the banks that were "too big to fail" has skewed the value system on pay equity. Yes, it may be fair that if you take the risks, you should enjoy the rewards, but when banks take the risk and fail, then *No!* their senior executive should not benefit from public funds used to write off their debts. Unfortunately, the financial "gang that couldn't shoot straight" seems to be back in the leadership role with US and Canadian banks again making record profits with CEO pay packets increasing. It seems that little has changed in the rate of risk and reward for performance.

Nobel Prize-winning economist Joseph Stiglitz, in his book, *Free Fall,* cuts through causes or lessons learned to astutely summarize that greed played the largest role in the crisis. The expectations of society were sacrificed for the benefit of the insiders. I'm not convinced that a lot has changed since in this regard. *JPMorgan* Chase, *Citigroup*, *Barclays* and *The Royal Bank of Scotland* pleaded guilty to rigging the world's currency market from 2007 – 2013 as reported in the Associated Press in 2015. They will pay more than $5 billion in penalties.

Erosion of Values

Unethical behavior does not occur overnight. It is a steady erosion of personal conduct where what is acceptable or not acceptable is no longer distinguishable. Research at Harvard University by Professor Max Bazerman with author and Professor Francesca Gino, states that, "once the ethical line has been crossed, an institutionalization of corruption can occur in which unethical acts become a part of daily activities and people often have a vested interest in remaining quiet."[1]

Unequivocally their research shows that incremental steps of unethical behavior largely go unnoticed. This may cause individuals to escalate unethical activities with no particular malice to defraud until it must be dealt with. As we have seen, some companies choose to hide the issues until caught fearing that they will hurt the brand, while others take actions such as firing those who perpetuate moral or illegal acts and distance themselves immediately with good reason.

For business people it is worth remembering how quickly organizations can become misguided in the pursuit of achieving their ends. Far too often, a corporate action comes down to: *Is it cheaper to obey or disobey?*

In September 2008, a former *Imperial Tobacco* employee admitted to a decade-long scheme of shipping tax-free cigarettes into the United

States where they would then be shipped back into Canada for sale by smugglers. The article states that Imperial controls 65% of the Canadian cigarette market and remits $6 billion dollars in annual duties and taxes. The scheme netted Imperial $600-700 million dollars per year. The fine for this illegal act was a mere 10% of the take: a small price to pay. Clearly it was cheaper to disobey.

The 2013 horrific collapse of the Rana Plaza in Bangladesh, which killed over 1100 factory workers, was where *Loblaw's Joe Fresh* clothing was produced. Although *Loblaw* had supplier codes of conduct in place, they had been sourcing from the illegally constructed factory for several years. While Loblaw has since committed to improving fire and building safety in Bangladesh factories, the lapse on its supply chain social responsibilities and limited corporate governance highlights a committed drive for profits over values.

Governance and Awareness

The previous examples remind us why the need for governance must go beyond simply being responsible to the shareholders. The expectations of society need also to be upheld as an equal factor in all decisions. This means that a transparency and an awareness of what is happening on all levels of production must be part of governance. It is only then, that you can use the value of many eyes to make good and "right" business decisions.

In example, because outsourcing and offshoring are major cost cutting strategies by global manufacturers, ethical accounting and awareness is crucial if anyone is expected to take a fair stance. This is why reviewing the record of corruption in various countries is appropriate. Using tools such as the *Transparency International*'s Corruption Perception Index helps companies become more aware of societal levels of corruption and be more on guard against the kinds of local conditions that lead to tragedies such as the one in Bangladesh.

When international or large corporations are guilty of unethical and illegal practices and are forced to go to court, we see it get wide media attention and the issues become transparent. However, the scandal sometimes misdirects the fact that many others in the market are also playing by their own rules. And, to add to that, the actual damage to an organization's image or brand is not always enough and does not always have long lasting negative results. In short, we cannot depend on the courts and media to govern. Business leaders and supply professionals have to be part of governance and awareness. They need to be vigilant in their dealings, to make sure they know more about their own systems and operations, including how products and services are promoted and brought to market. They need to take the lead and stand firm as corporately responsible citizens or conscious capitalists before the ethical path is lost in the jungle of greed.

The Political Imperative

In Canada, the impetus for a stronger commitment to sustainability took place with the lead up to and the awarding of the 2010 Olympic and Paralympic Games to the City of Vancouver in June 2003. Mayor Larry Campbell made public pronouncements to ensure a legacy that would benefit the local communities and included disenfranchised people.

Councilors, Tim Louis and Raymond Louie, took up the cause in the form of a council motion to implement an ethical and sustainable purchasing policy. The policy was a first in Canada and was aimed at fair trade agricultural products as well as clothing and uniform purchases. This came with great angst from the civic administration but exuberant support from the Non-Government Organizations (NGOs) that the Olympic Committee was committed to work with.

The administration saw this motion as making it unaffordable to meet their policy objectives. However, NGOs such as the *Maquila Solidarity Network,* felt that Vancouver would make such a difference that other civic entities across Canada would quickly follow suit. What was the result? In fact, the policy did achieve an awareness that was not present before. Ethical purchasing policies are growing in acceptance and continue to be adopted across North America by many private and public sector organizations. While political imperatives may have to be coaxed through, they are worth it when the stakeholders return to what is the right thing to do or what is ethical.

Why Be Ethical?

What is the pursuit of the bottom line if it is not to make the most possible profit—in other words: greed? Ethical responsibility in enterprise clearly flies in the face of greed. In the name of making a profit, how do we protect against greed spiraling out of control as it has so many times in the recent past? Being ethical means taking an active stand so that everyone is on guard to prevent an erosion of values. It means bringing mindfulness of the global impacts of doing business and rewarding good governance. We have to set it as the standard not just for private enterprise but also within our political machinery.

Private and public sector organizations often announce that they have a policy around CSR or sustainability as soon as possible as it makes them look good. However, it often takes a substantial amount of time before we see these changes in effect as policy announcements generally precede actual commitments. This is where the difference of true commitment versus lip service or what we call "greenwashing" enters the picture.

Why be ethical? I once asked Toby Barazzuol, the founder of *Eclipse Awards International Inc.,* based in Vancouver, why he does so much for the community and his response was, "It's just the right thing to do." Simple. Direct. Sincere.

Not everyone still gets it so simply, which is why I have put together nine compelling reasons where corporate management can benefit by embracing sustainability practices.

 Nine Reasons for Engaging in Sustainability

With the Comprehensive European Trade Agreement pending between the US, Canada and Europe, it is wise to become informed of European sustainability values as they provide exemplary leading practices and mistakes that we can learn from. The following nine reasons for engaging in sustainability were developed from the leading ideas and practices, not merely from theories and give us the key reasons enterprise leaders should embrace sustainability practices.

1. Improves Corporate Image and Brand Reputation
2. Creates an Even Playing Field
3. Encourages the Efficient Use of Resources for International Business
4. Reduces the Depletion (and Extinction) of Natural Resources
5. Attracts and Retains Employees

6. Avoids Dependency on Oil-based Products
7. Reduces Operating Costs (and/or Increases Profits)
8. Balances Social Wealth to Social Well-being
9. Increases Sales and Loyalty

#1 Reason
Improves Corporate Image and Brand Reputation

Corporate infractions have made front page news bringing seriously negative press to a company's image. Unfortunately, this bad press appears to be mostly short-term in its duration. On the other hand, do corporations actually benefit by being more responsible? That seems to be more of a mixed bag.

The 1989 *Exxon Valdez* oil spill off Alaska led to $5 billion in punitive damages being awarded in 1994. However, in 2008, this was reduced to compensatory damages of $507.5 million dollars following a record $40.6 billion year by *Exxon Mobil* the year before. While they may have been despised in the short-term, in the long-term the public forgot them. Does this mean the public forgave them?

It appears that things have changed and people are less forgiving. *BP's* infamous 2010 oil spill in the Gulf of Mexico will remain etched in memory for decades to come. The disaster allegedly resulted from operational shortcomings involving *BP* and several subcontractors. Now the company must deal with serious financial issues in order to survive in the market while the image and brand reputation of *BP* may never recover to its former stature. This disastrous event also cast a shadow on other oil industry operators. *BP*, for its size and previous CSR market reputation is the embodiment of *not* meeting the expectations of society.

Certainly many companies do position themselves to be positively aligned to CSR values and practice such as: *Patagonia, Seventh Generation, Starbucks, Stonyfield Farm, IKEA, Van City Savings Credit Union, Green and Black, Ben and Jerry's Ice Cream, Mountain Equipment Co-op and Unilever.*

Consistently paying attention to corporate values and market acceptance contributes to a positive image and brand. Companies that have an effective sponsorship and philanthropic program in place can improve their image and product lineup through complementary strategies, though that should never be the main reason as both the public and the employees can smell the difference.

 ## #2 Reason
Creates an Even Playing Field
for International Business

The idea is that if manufacturing facilities in two countries both practice CSR, their respective societies will benefit. For example, corporations that endorsed ISO standards created an even playing field when they adopted common quality standards. It was an important step leading to effective energy management. Standards not only provide methodology, they also provide a benchmark of comparison to improve performance.

The benefits of the ISO 50001 on Energy are:
- A framework for integrating energy efficiency into management practices
- Making better use of existing energy-consuming assets
- Benchmarking, measuring, documenting, and reporting energy intensity improvements and their projected impact on reductions in Green House Gas (GHG) emissions

- Transparency and communication on the management of energy resources
- Energy management best practices and good energy management behaviors
- Evaluating and prioritizing the implementation of new energy-efficient technologies
- A framework for promoting energy efficiency throughout the supply chain
- Energy management improvements in the context of GHG emission reduction projects

The adoption of stringent standards and laws directed at human rights and environmental protection are ways in which businesses compete as market leaders by having standards they meet be seen as the benchmark for others. Conversely, other players in the market are reluctant to invest in higher standards while trying to build market share. For example, ISO 633:2007 defines cork as a raw material for the industry as well as the terms to be used in describing the different forms in which cork may be found. While a larger international company may be able to afford to comply with this specification, a smaller producer may not. This could limit the latter's access to market opportunities which favours the former.

Most countries have agreed to improve the environmental and human rights standards of the companies that operate within their borders. Others continue to use the gaps to their strategic advantage and probably won't change until revenue losses (or laws) force them to reevaluate their business model. However, consider the fact that countries that produce a more expensive product are not necessarily behind countries that produce cheaper products. China and Germany both compete in producing mild steel, for example, but the more expensive German product— that is made following ISO (or higher) standards—is doing well in the market place. Germany has a very strong general economy and high standards, and yet can still compete. Its global thinking has tended to help them in the long run.

Recently, two progressive companies have skillfully handled the controversy around human rights practices when using Chinese labor. *Patagonia*, a well respected outdoor sporting clothing gear company, knowingly does business with factories in China in order to remain competitive, however, they refuse to support factories that employ children under the approved age set by the *International Labour Organization* (ILO). They also work directly with NGOs and other brand managers to affect change in China.

Similarly, *Mountain Equipment Co-op* does a lot of product sourcing out of China. While acknowledging the deplorable government record on human rights, *Mountain Equipment Co-op* works to find factories that demonstrate a commitment to improving workers' rights. They choose to engage with China's entrepreneurs and educate them about global practices. *Mountain Equipment Co-op*'s due diligence has uncovered and reported on cases of worker abuse while also taking proactive steps towards reversing the abuses.

3 Reason
Encourages the Efficient Use of Resources

Enlightened, sustainable thinkers recognize opportunities for more efficient resource usages that can give them a significant advantage over other companies. Compact fluorescent lights, for example, use less energy but also contain mercury that ends up in landfills when the lights are discarded. Some compact fluorescent manufacturing companies recognized this and initiated their own recycling campaigns (often dropping off new supplies and picking up the old). Consequently they created a mercury supply source through their recycling programs that also allows them to use resources more efficiently.

Innovative technologies have allowed industries to act more responsibly while remaining profitable. For example, incineration was once the way industries and cities dealt with waste. The resulting emissions were considered harmful and wasteful. With today's changes in technology, however, incineration is again being explored as a means of dealing with waste as it's now possible to safely divide and recover resources, mitigate harmful exhausts, and also reclaim the energy used in doing this.

 ## #4 Reason
Reduces the Depletion (and Extinction)
of Natural Resources

Supply professionals have the greatest impact on reducing the depletion and extinction of natural resources, resources they will need in the future. They need to be aware of alternative products and services that will encourage sustainability. They also need to know what products or services are currently in development. Yet, they must not get pre-sold on new products and services by the simple marketing of them (see Greenwashing later under *How*). There can be many pros and cons, plus short and long-term benefits of product choices that require further investigation before making a final purchasing or contractual decision.

Simple choices such as buying copy that is 30% Post Consumer Waste (PCW) content copy paper instead of virgin copy paper can create debate. Some staff will want to buy 100% PCW paper instead. Recent studies at University of British Columbia and the University of Calgary do not support buying 100% PCW paper. The increased cost exceeds the relative value of the environmental benefits. The better decision is to buy 30% PCW paper and *reduce* the consumption of paper. There is also the option of negotiating better pricing on 30% PCW content to get a cheaper comparable price to that of virgin paper through commitments to buy in volume.

Yet, not all decisions to preserve resources are simply making good choices in what to buy. As reported by my colleague Victoria Wakefield of UBC, "I was inspired by an article by Basil Waugh[2] on going paperless to better control the paper waste in the area I managed. Our courier/freight staff was printing between 800 and 1000 sheets, double-sided each month. Often, we were printing PDF copies of waybills for our monthly billing and record retention requirements. When printing PDFs the printer becomes frozen to other users. This is very inconvenient, a waste of time, and created a regular gripe among the office staff.

We enlisted the help of IT to show us how to sort, store and effectively catalogue our records electronically. IT set up courier/freight with a dedicated hard drive and some guidelines on data sorting and storage. In addition, we added software to be able to make comments and notations into the PDFs. In turn, this allows for electronic communication to the campus community, which eliminated the printing of billing and statement requests.

The success of paperless billing allowed us to become confident in implementing other paperless systems. We no longer had the office copier that prints faxes. The device had a set up function that allows the fax to go straight to email. This was another very simple adjustment that involved the assistance of the copier service technician and in-house IT staff. We then expanded our paperless office initiatives to include journal vouchers and requisitions, previously done on two-part NCR paper, which is expensive. We took the image and recreated it as a Word document. Going paperless saves time, money and trees. While many larger companies may be creating these systems now, many smaller, and dare I say it, lazier companies are not bothering, or are not backing it up with proper training."

5 Reason
Attracts and Retains Employees

The greater affinity people have for working with companies that support CSR values, the greater the attraction and retention of great employees. Companies such as *Timberland* and *Merck* claim this is a key component of their human resources strategy. Many of the organizations that use sustainability as a tool to enhance their image and brand also see the strategic value of designing their human resources selection process to address staffing needs. CSR companies enjoy a halo effect where they can align their corporate values to their employee values. Employees then become *community ambassadors*, which has an even stronger positive effect on the corporate image and brand.

Reducing staff turn over contributes to a more profitable organization. Aligning HR strategies with personal values and customer expectations is a win-win-win.

#6 Reason
Avoids Dependency on Oil-based Products

Is avoiding dependency on oil-based products CSR or just good business? The answer is right on both counts. If supply chains can deliver cost effective alternatives to current oil-based products, these are more likely to be well accepted and increase demand. Yet, beware of unintended consequences. The conversion of corn to biodiesel, for example, could go down as one of the biggest blunders of all. The displacement of imported oil for fuel with corn-based fuel has unintentionally created bigger social problems. Corn-based fuel is often responsible for driving the cost of food up in places most in need of inexpensive food.

A successful example of disruptive technology in the area of an alternative to fossil fuel is the concept of the solid-oxide fuel cells developed by *Bloom Energy*. These low-emission, super-efficient, devices are independent of the conventional energy grid. *Bloom* developed their Energy Server™ technology for leading customers such as *Google*, *Staples*, *eBay*, *Walmart*, *FedEx*, *Coca Cola* and others.

Will the so-called "Bloom Box" be the answer to future energy supplies? It certainly appears to be a scalable model that can run on an agnostic fuel source including plant waste or natural gas. This could have real impact in developing countries especially where grids are lacking or fractured. By powering the fuel cells on indigenous materials or waste the *Bloom* technology has taken a big step away from fossil fuel dependency.

#7 Reason
Reduces Operating Costs (and/or Increases Profits)

Reducing operating costs or increasing profits is what business is all about, however, when looking at budgets from a CSR perspective we need to build that in as well. The perception that sustainable products or services will cost more is often taken out of context. They are usually compared to traditional products based solely on the acquisition cost and fail to take into account the longer-term benefits.

Unfortunately, it is often what "everyone else is doing" that determines purchasing decisions as there is less risk professionally and personally in sticking to conventional items. It's a *best practices* scenario prevailing over *leading practices*.

For example, in Flin Flon, Manitoba, a zinc mining company faces the unenviable task of trying to maintain the integrity of its concrete chambers that are subjected to the harshest conditions. Every two to three years the concrete must be reconditioned to maintain its functional integrity. Currently this costs millions of dollars in replacement and disposal problems. The mine operator needs a more effective and responsible solution to this ongoing problem.

Along comes *Protocol Environmental Solutions* who has formulated a unique line of InnerCrete™ Membrane Technology products that treat and prevent the very problems the mine was experiencing. Even better, Protocol's ICP products are sustainable, chemically modifying and consolidating the concrete through an inorganic reaction with the latent materials present in the concrete mass. These products contain no volatile organic compounds, are non-hazardous, and are fully biodegradable, nor are they dependent on oil-based materials. If the cost of the product is a little more at the front end, but reduces a lot of hassle and expense on the back end, it is a win-win situation.

Supply professionals who take a pragmatic approach can demonstrate both hard and soft cost savings through innovative technologies and products and services that support sustainability principles. Responsibly introducing green products can still protect the bottom line, and introducing products or services that are more sustainable and support a company's CSR strategy can easily be managed while ensuring profitability.

 ## #8 Reason
Balances Social Wealth to Social Well-being

The richest 1% of the world (50 million people) receives as much income as the bottom 57% (2.7 billion people) with 13% of the world's population undernourished despite the fact that the world produces sufficient food to meet everyone's required daily caloric needs.
~ Patrima Bansal, Canada Research Chair in Business Sustainability

The distribution of wealth is a contentious business issue, especially on a global scale. More and more businesses in emerging and 3rd world economies are demanding a greater share of the wealth that is created. Often they are producing goods at 1/10th the cost of production in North America, yet the workers themselves may not be receiving an equitable share, and indeed are not benefiting from better working conditions.

Improving the health of workers and society reduces the long-term costs associated with treating advanced health problems. Improving the quality of education builds the social capital, which is the source of the next generation of business leadership. It befits all companies to contribute to building stronger societies and helping to shape health and education standards for the populations they work with. Whether through their ability to support social development and working standards initiatives, by paying appropriate taxes (rather than avoiding them), or through direct investment, they have a responsibility to step up. This is not only a responsibility but also smart. It ensures a future for their workers, their worker's children, as well as their own.

It has also been proven time and time again that the higher the standard of living, and the greater the commitment to social investment, then the more stable and healthy an economy is overall. We can look an industry in the next example that has been severely exploited in the past, but through the leadership of a Foundation is trying to get companies on board towards that stability.

The World Cocoa Foundation (WCF) created an international network of governmental agencies, NGOs, foundations, and farmers to improve the sustainable development of cocoa as well as improving the health and education of workers. *The International Cocoa Initiative* (ICI) focuses on the elimination of child and forced labor in West Africa, one of the largest cocoa producing areas. The WCF and major ICI companies, including *Cargill*, *Kraft*, and *Nestlé*, are working together for more responsible business practices and agricultural methods. Similarly, efforts in Belize by the *Fairtrade Foundation* help to ensure sustainable cocoa practices.

The progressive retailer *Green & Black* has been sourcing organic cocoa from Belize since 1994. *Mars Incorporated* announced in 2009 it is targeting to provide sustainably sourced cocoa by 2020. Although a few other major brands of chocolate products have been slow to adopt more responsible practices it appears that the shift has begun in this market sector.

#9 Reason
Increases Sales and Loyalty

As organizations take on more sustainable product and service offerings, one should see a correlation in increased sales due to customer loyalty. The companies who build a brand preference for their sustainable products often are able to attract strong customer loyalty. *Newman's Own* and *Mountain Equipment Coop* and *Clorox's* Greenworks™ products, are examples. And, just like other practices in business, the first ones to use *leading practices* are the ones remembered.

As mentioned before, both the public and the employees can smell the difference of a company that is sincere (or one that does lip service), and this determines their loyalty level. It is also increasingly easy to research companies via the Internet and social media around company practices. An increasing percentage of consumers will be buying accordingly. If one considers reviewing services like *Yelp*, that has changed many local businesses by getting good reviews (or bad ones), we see that the marketing spin of companies will only go so far. Even *Amazon* product reviews, has knowledgeable consumers leading other consumers. It is foreseeable, and already happening, that these reviewers will more and more include the knowledge of whether a company is creating sustainable products and services.

If your reason to implement CSR needs no further justification than greater consumer loyalty, then you have it.

How to Use the Reasons

Out of all the reasons you only need to find one compelling enough to convince decision-makers that your organization must include CSR. All the other reasons are simply the cream.

Pick Your Most Compelling Reason:
- Improves Corporate Image and Brand Reputation
- Creates an Even Playing Field for International Business
- Encourages the Efficient Use of Resources
- Reduces the Depletion (and Extinction) of Natural Resources
- Attracts and Retains Employees
- Avoids Dependency on Oil-based Products
- Reduces Operating Costs (and/or Increase Profits)
- Balances Social Wealth to Social Well-being
- Increases Sales and Loyalty

If these reasons do not have enough urgency for you, or your colleagues, then let us answer the question, *Why Now?*

Why Now?

Al Gore's documentary, *An Inconvenient Truth*, raised public awareness of the threats to our planet due to climate change. Leading scientists are saying in no uncertain terms that unless we act quickly the earth will become a Venus: shrouded in a saturated CO_2 bubble, unable to sustain life. While there are many disbelievers who debate the magnitude of climate change, the solutions make sense whether the problem is as great as feared or not. If we can reduce green house gases, conserve energy, water and natural resources, reuse waste energy, reduce landfill waste, utilize renewable energy, consume less fuel, live healthier, and pass the planet along in good condition–why shouldn't we?

And yet, all of our economic models that set pricing for food, clothing, cars, entertainment, and shelter are predicated on low fossil fuel prices lasting for many more decades. Quite simply, the environment cannot continue to absorb the massive emissions our lifestyle is creating without adjusting temperatures.

Unfortunately, the misinformation swirling around climate change has been seen as a signal to slow down the momentum towards sustainability and even pull a U-turn. The weakening global economies of post 2009 have been an excuse for diluting attention from anything that is not directly aimed at pure profit or job creation generation. The truth is that more sustainable business models mean that companies will actually consume fewer resources, emit fewer emissions, reduce the use of toxic chemicals, build healthier communities, protect the biosphere, create different kinds of jobs and still contribute to the bottom line.

The subject continues to polarize conversations between advocates and antagonists. The terms *corporate social responsibility* or *sustainability* are tossed around without a full understanding of what they really mean. Often they are used as idealistic beacons whereas they can also refer to the practice and implementation of sound stewardship principles.

Properly implemented, CSR will find the common ground that enables investments to continue, goods to be produced, and communities to share the proceeds that support an educated and healthy planet. By sharing ideas that work we will be able to overcome barriers and advance sooner rather than later. We need to *create* value rather than make claims to value.

The new frontier lies in the commercialization of energy alternatives. Current business models rely on conventional fossil fuel costs. We can reduce emissions—that *isn't* the problem. Doing it within an economic model which transitions us to more sustainable energy sources *is* the challenge. Our current power distribution grids are based on fossil fuel and hydropower and there can be formidable entry costs in bringing non-fossil fuels to the grid for mass accessibility.

Remember that urgency for change now always comes with push back. There is the NIMBY phenomenon – Not In My Backyard. Wind farms may appear unsightly to a natural desert landscape or to ocean front properties which generate fears that the sight of the huge tri-bladed generators will drive down property values. It is interesting to note that there was an identical reaction to the first gasoline stations which popped up next to livery stables. We got used to it. No one really wants to accept radical changes but they do want to have sustainable, safe, and reliable sources of energy. They just don't like paying extra for the benefits, even when the benefits secure their future and their children's.

In the coming years, climate change will affect all sourcing decisions. Natural resources such as lumber, coffee, or fish stocks, for example, will undoubtedly adapt but will their availability remain abundant in their current locales? Crop yields will likely shift with temperatures and water levels. Storm surges will reshape coastlines and socio-economic activities. Floods will carve the landscape and force economic sustainability studies.

Hurricane Katrina changed the commercial and recreational fishing industries dramatically and made insurance companies very nervous and madly revising their policies and rates. But, in truth, there may be no better protection than our initiative to plan and make changes. We will need to do some crystal ball gazing to see how, when and where sourcing strategies will be affected through climate change-related patterns.

Like labor disputes, I believe that we will eventually find a resolution that fits the needs of all parties. It is human nature to delay looking for answers while we think we can afford to wait. We will only start to see a mutual benefit when the resolve of all players is tested and they begin to notice that the resources are starting to shrink.

What should be keeping us up at night is when. When will all these changes start to happen? To contribute to the well-being of the planet, and ensure all communities support only businesses that are socially responsible, the answer can only be: **NOW.**

Who?

Who?

Never doubt that a small group of thoughtful, committed,
citizens can change the world. Indeed, it is the only thing that ever has.
~ Margaret Mead

I have identified seven major groups that need to lead the charge for Corporate Social Responsibility and fearlessly ensure that we will have sustainability in all our methods as soon as possible. These groups are:

1. Supply Chain Managers (SCM) or Supply Chain Professionals at all levels
2. Entrepreneurs and Social Entrepreneurship
3. Third-Party Audit Organizations
4. Non-Government Organizations
5. Government—from City to Federal
6. Philanthropists and Sponsors
7. Consumers

If all of these groups and as individuals exert their power to take action, we will eventually accept CSR practices and principles as second nature. Routines will be as acceptable and normal as the normal maintenance we do around our cars and homes to insure better and safer futures, like buckling up a seat belt and installing fire alarms and testing them.

In this section on *Who*, I will go into each of these roles and hopefully not only enlighten you as to the possibilities and impact of each on the road to full sustainability for our planet, but also show how they can often work even better in conjunction with each other. People also need to know what the leading practices are, as well as what has not worked and what history we can learn from. To that end, be sure we will be showing many examples you can draw inspiration from, learn from the pitfalls, as well as use as direct resources.

Of all the previous groups listed that can lead the charge to CSR, supply chain management is the group of professionals I both identify with and want to inspire. They are uniquely positioned to educate entrepreneurs about the practical possibilities instead of just thinking short-term bottom-line. They make the decisions that affect patterns of buying in the largest quantities. They are the ones who can think about sourcing and resources in an out-of-the-box way. For all those reasons, let's start with looking at the role of supply chain managers and how that is changing.

 The Changing Role of Supply Professionals

The supply chain is the common denominator in all businesses. The expanded role of responsibility for supply professionals including purchasers, buyers, planners, logistics managers, inventory specialists, materials analysts, operations managers and many other titles and roles, is taking place across the globe. Where we may be thinking domestic market, we are certainly playing within a global market. The supply practices in Vancouver, Canada; Chicago, USA; and Mumbai, India are now connected. The exchange between the buyers and sellers is becoming a shared responsibility to be inclusive of social values and cognitive of environmental consequences that affect our shared planet.

This shared responsibility requires a business strategy and a tactical execution. Supply professionals need to be aware of the issues relevant to their organization and to its supply partners for goods and services. It is a time for a renewal of strategies that will allow us to prosper within the existing finite resources.

Thirty years ago business was looking for leadership to address the environmental movement. Supply management was not ready to take it on. Buyers were largely consumed in their zeal to drive down the incremental costs of whatever they had to buy for their respective organizations— inflation was upper most in their minds. In fairness, the environmental interest was co-opted by advocates like *Greenpeace* and the response from business was to ride it out and hope they would go away.

Eventually senior management hired strategists to find the middle ground to deal with the environmental issues in order to preserve profitability. This is what happened. The strategists were not from supply management. They were from the other business disciplines because supply management was not at the table for the discussions. The belief was: *We'll figure it out and tell purchasing what to do.* Subsequently the engineers and marketing crowd developed new specifications to send down to purchasing in the form of requisitions to be filled. Purchasing staff were not as up to speed on the environmental matters so they deferred to other disciplines for guidance and slowly started to learn a few things. Environmental issues are now well-established on corporate agendas and supply managers are becoming effective at factoring in the environmental concerns when making supply decisions, but is that leading? Businesses are led by individuals, and like any social change it will be a number of progressive individuals with a common vision that will drive the change towards responsible business practices.

The rapidly emerging story today is about sustainability and corporate social responsibility. Where are organizations looking for answers? To supply management professionals. This recognizes and acknowledges the value that companies receive when supply professionals act responsively to the changing needs in the market. This new role is a juxtaposition of the economic and environmental issues while meeting the expectations of stakeholders and customers. Using the analogy of a product life cycle for a professional standing, this is the time for supply-minded individuals to rebrand themselves. Retrospectively, in a few years, people will look back at this as the pivotal moment when supply professionals were asked to stand up or step aside.

To affect change in business decisions involving the acquisition of goods, services, and equipment, the cognitive task is to see sustainability as an outcome of sound judgment. Successfully implementing the change strategy is the managerial role for supply professionals. This requires making sustainability an inherent part of its decision-making responsibility. Interpreting the plethora of information and data surrounding sustainability and applying it to the values of the organization is the challenge. That is the strategic imperative that supply managers must get their head around first. This puts them in control of their destiny.

To date the focus has been on developing the leanest and most efficient supply chain to drive down the costs or to increase the profitability. We have always trained people on the *economic* values, which are an outcome of commerce. In the last 30 years we have now shown a concern for the *environment* values. We are now layering the expectations of society on these two factors, environment and economic, to create a sustainable value proposition.

There are two emerging game changer strategies that supply chain professionals should actively consider to bring these values together that go beyond simply buying sustainable products and services.

The first game changer is about suppliers—the factor every supply chain professional needs in order to do their job. Ask yourself, what motivates suppliers to do their best for their client companies, and also follow those companies' standards and values beyond simply delivering a product? Outsourced suppliers is the norm, but it is new ideas which are seeing them being transformed into insourced suppliers. Rather than paying for services or goods to be manufactured by the lowest cost provider, instead some companies create a new working relationship where the service provider becomes part of the parent organization. It creates the psychological contract of an employee relationship as opposed to simply being a contractor for hire. This is part of the movement towards distributed organizations. This allows for greater control and commitment for the long-term sustainability values, while retaining some of the benefits of outsourcing.

The UK company *Quickstart Global* has 600 staff operating in seven countries enabling start up companies to focus on their core strengths and scale up. *Quickstart* locates highly qualified people to fill the necessary positions for client companies wherever they reside. The client directly manages the globally recruited staff which works exclusively for the client.

Quickstart look after the legal and administration side of the business on behalf of its clients.

Monumental Games has used the insourcing model to grow its business. Founded in 2005 by Rik Alexander, Monumental finds great value in recruiting software designers out of India to find the best talent. Another UK company that is leveraging this business proposition is *Clear Cell*, a client of *Quickstart*.

Why is this important for sustainability for Supply Chain Managers (SCM) to have their suppliers inside? This model creates an incentive for the organizations to grow based on mutual benefits and makes it easier to join the environmental and social values to the economic values.

The next game changer in supply chains is supply chain finance. This strategy is aimed at eliminating the importers and going instead directly from source to brand manager retailers. The focus is on cost reduction and inventory reduction. When going through an importer the social issues at source community and country are often lost in the zeal to find the lowest cost producer. The strategy of buying in container loads is to get the lowest unit price, often ignoring other factors. Supply chain finance is a relatively new method of conducting international transactions. Using a standard technology platform, all partners in a trade can follow the entire transaction from order to fulfillment and payment. This allows multi national organizations to source from small medium enterprises around the world – without a middleman. This significantly reduces the cost of goods sold and provides access to a lower cost of capital. Supply chain finance allows smaller players to participate in the market where only larger companies had the opportunity. Service providers such as *Bolero, Capital Tool, Demica, Finacity, Orbian, Prime Revenue,* and *Trade Card* along with funding companies like *Citigroup, HSBC, Santander,* and *Wells Fargo* are leading the pack.

Supply chain professionals need to be aware and be able to make their cases for looking at source in order to take long-term care of that source. It is no longer acceptable to offload externality costs—the costs that follow cheap but unconscionable and harmful products and services—on to society – whether it is local or global – in order to create wealth. Supply chain professionals need to be the leaders to point out that profits are only as important as the means of attaining them.

Exploitive practices have been allowed by every nation at some time in its history and, unfortunately, this is still present today, but it is being challenged aggressively on many fronts. China is being criticized for not addressing its human rights in a more progressive manner and timetable. China has become the elephant in everyone's living room – for all of the good reasons and the bad reasons. Darfur continues to experience atrocities and oil has been discovered to exacerbate the untenable situation. Someone will always look the other way to get at cheaper oil or other natural resources at a lower price. China is reportedly trading for oil in the Sudan region. Shame on them—and us—for purchasing this oil.

Bringing suppliers inside in order to take long term care of the source and the community it exists in, are game changers because they require a higher level of leadership and operations decision-making. All SCM should be working towards this level. But equally important is the attention paid to everyday cost-of-business purchases and who is doing the purchasing.

Lesser attention has been paid to the maintenance, operating and repair types of purchases, known as MOR. These decisions have primarily been made on short-term cost/benefit analyses. In many industries these can account for a higher percentage of the budget than capital projects. Where capital projects occur with less frequency, operational buys occur daily over decades. MOR buys are often made by end user employees, thereby bypassing values and professional scrutiny. This is an area where supply professionals need to devote their talent, interrupt the norms and engage end users in their organization and give them options that include sustainable products and services.

Energy conservation is a key strategy in most organizations. Utility bills used to be largely ignored and were simply a part of the cost of doing business. As energy costs increased, attention was given to being much more resourceful and creative with energy consumption. Natural gas has grown to be a more competitive and plentiful source of fuel. However, the fracking method used to release the natural gas from the rock formations is questionable. Is it a reasonable compromise? No. And someone needs to understand and speak up about it, and that is the supply professional.

Supply professionals must secure goods and services required. This can work in tandem with creating long-term strategies that includes conducting market intelligence, seeking better options to address an expanded definition of their role, and as being uncompromising as possible towards sustainability. Supply professionals also are going to want to work with their suppliers to develop new standards, (which is easier if you have pulled them inside the organization).

When supply management membership in the C-Suite club (among the CEOs, COOs, CFOs, etc.) becomes more numerous, only then will supply chains be seen as more strategic in terms of affecting change in responsible practices. Change seldom happens as quickly as some would like – and happens too fast for many to make the transition. For too long we have been focused on simply *doing the same things right* and we are now in the transition of *doing the right things.* My sense of optimism says that now is the time for supply chain professionals to be the leaders.

 ## Entrepreneurship Can Create Value

Here I want to show why small and medium business owners and social enterprises are also be leading the charge for CSR. It's not a coincidence that resilient economies are a common attribute in western societies where we have greater democracy and social values. Our democratic pursuits and social values are vital to a healthy society. At the heart of the economic activity are small and medium-sized enterprises (SMEs) which provide goods and services.

SMEs, defined as up to 500 employees, account for 98% of all the companies in Canada and 99.7% in the US[3] They have created over 77% of the new jobs in the past decade. SMEs are typically owned and operated by the people that live within the local communities and use local goods, services and create employment opportunities. SMEs support the local sports teams, local arts and entertainment, as well as governmental infrastructure, health and education, through taxes, their own sponsorship, and the direct spending of their employees.

Social Enterprise (SE) focuses on achieving measurable social, cultural, and environmental objectives through their services and products. SEs are not charities. They add to the economy by providing meaningful work reducing the burden on governmental assistance programs. Individuals working for SEs also spend a good portion of their wages locally. The presence of SEs emerged as to counter balance exploitive business practices and inequities in the distribution of wealth. SEs can control large amounts of capital but surplus funds return directly to the community. Common not-for-profit SEs are credit unions and cooperatives.

Some Social Enterprises with long, successful histories that have become larger enterprises are:

- *Mountain Equipment Co-op,* since 1970s
- *Blue Cross Blue Shield* Health Care Insurers, since 1930s
- *Van City Savings Credit Union,* since 1940s
- *PARC (Providing Advocacy and Recognizing Capabilities),* since 1950s
- *AAA American Automobile Association and many state* and provincial auto associations, such as BCAA, since 1900s are now primary insurers for their large membership
- *Car Co-ops such as Modo,* a nonprofit car sharing organization in Vancouver that stimulated with its success more car sharing organizations, both nonprofit and for-profit, since 1990s

Both Social Enterprises and Small to Medium Enterprises ensure a higher percentage of revenues being redistributed in the local economy. The 2013 *Power of Purchasing* report concluded that office supply SMEs redistribute 33% of their revenues locally compared to 17% with MNCs and that SMEs create twice as many jobs! SMEs can be as price competitive as MNCs.

The Silicon Valley arguably was an incubator for SMEs, creating new industries that spawned multi-national corporations. Many of these corporations continue to encourage innovation found through SMEs and contribute to CSR programs. However, corporations also initially championed the outsourcing of goods and services at the expense of domestic SMEs and SEs. Over reliance on outsourcing was found to be an unsustainable model due to the adverse effect on local or domestic economies.

CSR balances the need for purely profit-motivated strategies with the need for sustainable growth. SMEs and SEs together can be the conduits for sustaining social and economic values. However, having a "local address" is not sufficient to justify why a local business should get a contract. SMEs and SEs need to always make a business case for the three Ps: profitability, people and the planet. If they are upholding the value of those and can demonstrate it, more business should be placed at their doorstep.

Community-based businesses are as essential as multinational corporations. CSR requires that organizations develop strategies that are inclusive and diverse to ensure sustainable development.

For-profit SMEs which behave with CSR intentions throughout their business practices:
- *Patagonia (US)*—outdoor gear
- *Bovince Ltd. (UK)*—digital printing
- *Solegear (CDN)*—bio plastics

Still widely held is the argument that the sole aim of business is driving profits for its shareholders. And let's be clear: insufficient profits will drive companies out of business. However, profit making and being socially responsible are not binary decisions. There are many discretionary choices companies can take to start contributing to the solving the serious global problems we face.

Chances are, if you are reading this book, you are working for, or a member of at least one of these two groups (SME or SEs), and may have more influence than you realize over how they conduct business. For your benefit you may want to look at the example companies or review your organization and see if they are doing all they can to be leaders. Later on you can look at the *How* section of this book and recommend it to your supply chain professionals and other leaders as a template to begin. SMEs and SEs need to be leading the charge for CSR because they alone have the most impact, which can be even greater when they are working together.

Social Entities

One way for business to lead is to team with others that already are promoting CSR. Social entities are comprised of three groups: social enterprises, social entrepreneurs and social investors. For supply management the first two groups are excellent sources for goods and services that connect to the local community.

In Vancouver, the *Starworks Packaging and Assembly* organization provides great value for the services they provide while representing the interests of workers who have been marginalized for developmental disabilities. The workers are assured of minimum wages and benefits within a safe and supervised working environment. Outsourcing services to social entities, such as this, is relatively easy and makes good economic value. During times of labor shortages, these organizations can fill capacity constraints.

Deanne Ziebart, Director at *Starworks* believes in the CSR value system especially for supply chain, and says, "We are not asking that social purchasing be the primary mandate over price and quality, but that it be an additional criteria."

This has led to the social procurement model. Social procurement ensures domestic or local economic and social criteria are considered throughout the decision process. Social procurement favors localized sourcing while ensuring fair and open competition. LOCO BC and Buy Social Canada, an offshoot of the Buy Social UK organization, are drivers of local business and support social enterprises under the social procurement model. Social procurement can directly have a positive effect on health, crime rates and individual self-esteem, thereby mitigating community degradation.

David LePage from the *Enterprising Non Profits* organization talks about social enterprises as businesses that operate through nonprofits for the dual purpose of selling products and services *and* creating social value. He refers to this as the ripple effect. The ripple effect can be unintentional or intentional. A business will provide work for the social enterprise, or buy competitive goods or services from them. This enables these workers to improve their life and reduce their dependency on publicly funded social programs. Local businesses, in turn, benefit from stimulating the local economy. There is a reduction in social problems and a healthier community resulting from these agreements.

Small and medium businesses, teamed with social enterprises, can make a large difference in shaping the world and even forcing multinationals to join the CSR world we now must consider. They can and should lead the entrepreneurial charge towards what has been called conscious capitalism. They can do this by:

- Unbundling large contracts so that smaller social enterprises are able to supply a portion of the orders
- By encouraging larger sellers in the market to develop local sources using social entrepreneurs

- By distributing a list of preferred social enterprises for discretionary spending
- By employing local artists and performers for corporate gifting

As to the large corporations who claim a responsibility to make profits to its shareholders, we need to look at how to manage them and hold them to account. One way is through third party auditors.

 ## Third Party Audit Organizations

What are third party audit organizations? Third party certification or audit companies educate, control and govern policies, principles, best practices, certifications, standards, guidelines or legal requirements. Often these organizations are not-for-profits that charge for their services to develop their expertise and promote the use of their standards. The third party organizations that we are concerned with from a CSR perspective are comprised of a wide range from the obvious to the less obvious. This includes fair trade, organic certification and environmental organizations to sustainable building codes (LEED), and professional, worker-based and social organizations of all kinds. They are critical as to the checks and balances required when using sustainability criteria.

Third party certification is another way to set standards based on market readiness. Leading organizations in various industries and sectors recognize the value of third party certifications. For sellers, it sets a common standard and for buyers it allows them to assess the quality or effectiveness of products between competing brands. Third party certification as it applies to services or manufacturing conditions provides similar values to buyers and sellers in the same way that ISO standards or ILO conventions do. They set internationally recognized criteria as they have been researched and accepted in the market.

In the US there are multiple third party certifiers but *Fair Trade USA* is the largest. In Canada, there is primarily one organization, *TransFair Canada,* that can certify fair trade agricultural products such as coffee and many other products. Coffee retailers often use terminology such as *bird-friendly* or *frog-friendly* or *shade grown* to imply that their brand of coffee is meeting environmental and social standards. However, there is no way for the consumer to know this for certain unless it has the bona fide certification label, the trade mark of *TransFair,* on the packaging. Misleading labels and advertising do harm to those retailers that are in compliance with third party certification programs when compared to those who misrepresent their products or services. There is often a premium associated with fair trade certified products and unscrupulous sellers exploit that to their advantage when they are not in compliance. All buyers need to be aware of this, whether corporate or consumers and make the right decisions.

Another area where third party auditors have had an influence is to strongly endorse more responsible choices by fashion designers to use renewable materials in their clothing. Global designers are using animal-free products, bamboo fabrics, organic cottons, flax linens, fish skin fibers, hemp fibers, and soy fabrics. It's estimated that 80% of garments that are thrown out still have ¾ of their useful life. Textiles comprise 4% of landfill waste - a hidden cost of fast-fashion that has become externalized.

If individual fashion designers can be educated, and learn to work with the third party audit organizations, then why not all businesses and all individuals? Virtually all kinds of businesses can find a place to work with an appropriate third party to analyze their operations. Ideally, these organizations should be one of the first go-to spots when an organization (or individual) is thinking about CSR management. Being non-profits their fees are usually reasonable for services and they are happy to help, educate and guide with free information.

Third-party audit organizations keep abreast of what are the legal requirements and can help any members to become compliant with the laws and leading practices. They are also often the organizations that lobby our governments for controls with teeth. But what of our government, what is their role in leading CSR practices?

 ## Government's Role

Government at Federal, State or Provincial Levels

In October 2010, the Canadian government launched an education program aimed at nutritional values being added to the labels on foods. This is an outcome from the 2003 rules requiring food companies to provide this information. Although the companies did provide additional nutritional data it is only of help to the consumer if there is a standard of measurement to make an informed decision. It will be interesting to see how the companies comply with the spirit of the "per cent daily value" program.

While government expresses concern with nutritional values in foods, fast food chains are still making large profits. KFC (formerly *Kentucky Fried Chicken*) introduced their Double Down sandwich in 2010 and announced it was, "phenomenal for our KFC customers and our franchise partners across the country." The product contains 1740 milligrams of sodium which is by Canadian and USDA standards nearly a whole days recommended intake. It contains 32g of fat, 10g of which is saturated fats. Again, the daily-recommended limits for saturated fats are between 15 and 22 grams for a 2000 calorie a day diet. Introduced in the US in April 2010 and October in Canada, in its first month in the US market, sales were reported as more than 10 million units. In Canada sales were expected to be over 350,000 units in its first month. While it is hardly the worst of the junk food offenders, it did prove to us that marketers move fast food products, and governments are being pressured to get involved in the junk food debate.

There is a growing debate on the issue of taxing junk or snack foods. Michael Bloomberg tried an out and out ban on super sized sugary drinks in New York that stimulated the debate but also stimulated greater lawsuits and perhaps greater entrenchment from the marketers. A tax could be put towards offsetting health care costs linked to diabetes and obesity, as tobacco taxes are for their health-related links. These taxes are driven directly by the individual consumer. When Manitoba's Finance Minister and former advisor on health issues was asked about a *fat tax* he stated, "It's not something that actually achieves the goal of ensuring people make healthier food choices." This response sounds a little like an appeasement to the fast food retailers. The fat tax and possibly a sugar tax debates are not over and concerned consumers and health experts should keep the discussions going.

Consumers have an expectation that government oversight on various industries and practices is effective. If products are labeled responsibly then the consumers are informed at the source about the contents or attributes of the products they buy. Failure by government agencies to permit ambiguous product labels and claims leads to the lack of credibility and misinformation spread in the market. It undermines the confidence in consumers that business is serving the interests of society.

Our government officials, appointed to look into products (food products and all products) for health reasons respond to the pressure from their bosses, the taxpayers, but also their own financial backers and lobby groups. Ultimately government plays a critical role in determining how to legislate changes for the better and for all. While we depend on them, government's influence is always lagging in being a leading force, especially at the Federal level. However, there are opportunities that arise at the civic levels of governments that people should be looking to applaud and support.

Government at City Level

What did it mean for the City of Vancouver to become ethical purchasers? Here is an example. As a part of the due diligence on a potential contract for clothing, an evaluation team visited the local manufacturing sites. The team consisted of representatives from fire, health and safety, and supply management. They encountered one textile operation with rags covering the fire extinguishers and the fire exit padlocked, while another premise was filled with noxious fumes strong enough to cause two of the evaluation team members to feel nauseous and unable to drive their vehicles back from the site.

To their credit the two business owners within days responded to correct their respective situations. One cleaned up their discarded material pile and removed the padlock while the other spent $5000 dollars on an exhaust system. This owner subsequently sent a letter of thanks for pointing out what should have been an obvious health problem. Both business owners were successful in winning contracts with the City.

Without the policy in place, the likelihood representatives from the City would have made the site visits is highly unlikely. The traditional model has been to award to the lowest cost proponent, given that the quality was acceptable. In this instance, it was quite revealing as sweat shops and other unacceptable practices aren't always offshore. They are often in our own backyard – if we are looking for them.

Did it cost the City more? In fact, the cost of the goods covered under the contract was 35% lower based on a contract consolidation strategy to source these items. The reference to the consolidation strategy highlights the need that an ethical purchasing policy on its own will not achieve the intended results without an effective game plan. The game plan must be executed with multiple objectives being the goal. Succeeding on price without the social interests is not a win. Meeting the social aspects but over paying on price is not a win. The win in this situation was to deliver on both fronts.

While some argued that isn't the role of the City to inspect premises for safe working conditions and that other governmental agencies, such as *WorkSafe BC* are supposed to monitor working conditions and safety standards, the reality is that there are not enough inspectors to cover all of the potential businesses for these or other code violations. It is therefore the responsibility of supply management to execute due diligence and have a policy that holds them accountable.

Vancouver City's ethical purchasing policy was one of the first forays into the socio/economics relative to a common purchasing decision. These types of early wins are a great learning opportunity for supply professionals and others within an organization. Sharing the outcomes leads to expanding the scope, scalability, and staff aspirations.

The City of Edmonton was able to learn from Vancouver's mistakes and continued to leverage the opportunities with their policy. Unfortunately Vancouver's procurement group has not continued to be assertive in expanding their initial policy. This is an example of a passive policy adoption, whereby the policy becomes the *end* and not the *means*. However, in May 2010, with the 2010 Winter Olympics over, the City of Vancouver Council passed a motion to become the first major city in Canada to be a Fair Trade Town. There are over 800 cities in 19 countries with this status including London, Paris, and Rome. This movement reinforces the commitment cities need to adopt to favor Fair Trade certified agricultural products and extend support to handicrafts made by artisans.

Another role some government bodies are using is their own initiative to get funding for their community programs. The School Board of the City of Surrey in British Columbia has sought out more and more corporate sponsorships for its educational efforts, showing government a way to work with business to accomplish some goals (more on this under *Philanthropy, Sponsorship and Business*).

Government has its place in progressive initiatives, ethical procurement policies and of course, legislation, but even greater power can be seen in the operations and mandates of Non-Governmental Organizations (NGOs).

Non-Governmental Organizations (NGOs)

A life not lived for others is not a life.
~ Mother Theresa

NGOs, as self-appointed watchdogs, have successfully initiated change in social and environmental areas by working with businesses and government bodies. A number of these organizations made a critical impact on the planet for the health and care of the environment and for people. In the 1990s the former *World Wide Fund for Nature* took leadership in forming the *Forest Stewardship Council* and later the formation of the *Marine Stewardship Council* that operate in each individual country. Both these councils have done tremendous work in certifications and working with local industry to reduce harm and achieve sustainability. Their three goals are to foster environmentally appropriate, socially beneficial and economically viable actions.

The *Maquila Solidarity Network* (MSN) was formed in the 1990s to protect workers' rights in Latin America when US-based businesses outsourced assembly and production. MSN engaged with the elected officials in major cities across Canada (Vancouver, Ottawa, Calgary and Toronto), to promote sweatshop free clothing and the purchase of fair trade products by 2003. MSN acts on behalf of workers in many global locations. MSN has been quite successful with its strategies and often aligns itself with organized labor in the US and Canada and where multinational corporations have factory locations.

Business organizations should be familiar with local and international NGOs that focus on their market sector. Corporations are changing their tactics of ignoring or even fearing NGOs and are speaking with NGOs to hear their perspective on the issues that relate to the corporate operations and products. There can be apprehension when dealing with an NGO as their expectations and corporate agendas are not always in sync. NGOs engaging with a public or private sector entity often draw their respective suppliers into the net.

While most suppliers do not object to being held accountable they are uncomfortable with some of the requirements, which NGOs expect in supply agreements. They fear how others including their competition and labor unions may use their information. The information may include their factory locations and those of their own tier 1 and tier 2 suppliers. Suppliers that do not have affiliations with unionized labor may become targets of organizing campaigns even if they are fair employers. For buyers, this can potentially limit the number of suppliers.

Suppliers may also be tarred with the same brush whether they are good or bad. A trade embargo was applied to all companies operating in Myanmar in 2005. A Canadian clothing supplier who was operating in Myanmar and provided informal education and health benefits to its employees for over a decade was forced to close. Other related businesses within this jurisdiction, regardless of their compliance with ILO conventions, were subject to this trade embargo. This particular business relocated to Indonesia and continues to operate and provide voluntary education and health basics to its employees due to the personal commitment of the CEO.

Companies working with NGOs are still the best way to overcome any obstacles and move forward toward conscious capitalism. Active NGOs which business should be conscious of are: *Maquila Solidarity Network, Oxfam International, Amnesty International, Green Peace, World Wildlife Fund*, and the *Ethical Trading Action Group* (ETAG). The *Ethical Trading Action Group* is a Canadian coalition of faith, labor, teacher and non governmental. There are many other worthy NGOs. Please see a full list under Resources Page at the back of this book.

Faith-based NGOs such as the *Interfaith Center on Corporate Responsibility* (ICCR) were formed 30+ years ago to successfully protest the role of banks and other commercial interests operating in South Africa during the period of apartheid. Today the ICCR challenges the concentrated animal feeding operations, child labor on cotton harvesting, excessive CEO pay packets, affordable access to health care, entertainment industry standards, violence in video games, and many other social issues.

The relationships between NGOs and corporations can be positive and productive. There have been partnerships created through the expertise found in NGOs and the desire of corporate interests to develop new products and markets.

In 2008, *Clorox*, which successfully brands bleach and other consumer products, worked with the *Sierra Club* to launch its green line of cleaning products called Green Works™. This partnership has plans to include co-branding between the parties along with a revenue sharing formula.

This is a first for the *Sierra Club* and has been met with skepticism by some sustainability advocate groups and enthusiasm from others. The *Sierra Club* sees the agreement as a way to increase the availability of competitively priced green cleaning products to consumers. For *Clorox*, it is a gateway product into the green market and is an opportunity to leverage the marketing of its other products and brands.

Another successful, and previously unlikely, partnership was between *The Rainforest Alliance* and *Kraft Foods* to develop sustainable coffee production in Peru, Vietnam, and Columbia. This brings more niche coffee operations into the mainstream market. *Kraft* will provide funds to improve working conditions, buy more certified beans, and promote consumer awareness in its major markets. *The Rainforest Alliance* will monitor coffee farming operations with members of the *Sustainable Agricultural Network.*

Considering the success of these previously unheard of giants working with NGOs, there is no reason all businesses including the small and medium business owners can't work with NGOs. As previously mentioned in our *Why* section, this can give any business a shot in the arm for the sheer motivation and pride it gives employees and loyalty it gives consumers, not to mention, as an offshoot the positive public relations.

Beyond working with NGOs, is the possibility of working with full-fledged charities in many creative ways. They are in our *Who* section.

 ## Philanthropy, Sponsorship, and Business

In the U.S., for tax purposes, charities, non-profits and foundations are divided into three categories: Private, Exempt and Grantmaking. In Canada, it is similar with, Private Foundations, Public Foundations, and

Charitable organizations. There are 1.1 million such organizations in the U.S and 80,000 in Canada.

Where a company may find it difficult to adopt a more active CSR strategy, it can still do good through philanthropic or sponsorship participation. Companies can work with their supply chain partners and community groups to allocate resources other than checks in the form of time or other needed services. Volunteering for community programs can be encouraged by way of paid time off for staff members that choose to do so. A few hours a month can make a difference to the community organization and contribute to the company's morale.

Nancy Lee and Philip Kotler, authors of *Corporate Social Responsibility* and *Social Marketing: Influencing Behaviors for Good*, see a connection between philanthropy, sponsorship, and business leadership. The discretionary strategy proposed by Lee and Kotler in their book looks at strategically identifying with a specific cause and positioning the company to be recognized for its contributions of support for that cause. There may be direct or indirect benefits for the sponsoring company. They may enjoy increased revenues by being associated with the cause or it may enhance their community image. The point is the benefits are mutual and healthy.

Stonyfield Farms has participated in contributing to healthier foods, which contributes to a healthier community for 27+ years. They do this as a part of their corporate mission. *Stonyfield* partnered with *Danone* in Europe in 2006 to establish a larger organic food presence to create value and to educate consumers on healthier food choices. *Stonyfield* would receive direct and indirect benefits from this type of venture, which aligns with their corporate mission statement.

Sponsorship is less effective where a passive role does not have a strategic link to the overall corporate goals and objectives. A passive role often goes unnoticed by the staff of an organization and has less value when they do hear that a check was written for a local event. Staff does not have the experience of contributing as much as when they participate in a program that they see as "theirs." Not to dismiss giving but to develop a strategic philanthropic model may have a similar means but with a different effect.

There are examples where CSR is driven by the attraction of sponsorship rather than a philanthropic giving. Sponsorship is giving where there is an expectation that the company doing the giving will receive a tangible benefit. Using resources to influence others into favoring your organization either for its corporate image or for marketing and sales advantages is *not* philanthropy. This doesn't make sponsorship wrong. It is only wrong where sponsorship is a thin disguise for promotional purposes. Society needs corporate sponsorship and philanthropy.

A great example of CSR and philanthropy is in the story of *Bata Shoes*. The founder, Thomas Bata, practiced what he referred to as *responsible capitalism*. Bata adopted an apolitical philosophy of philanthropy in their global interests. They operate in Zimbabwe at a financial loss – they continue to operate and pay their employees in food and other benefits rather than simply shut down. Bata's wife, Sonja, is creating a sustainable community in the former company town of Batawa, Ontario as a part of her legacy. Giving, for the sake of giving.

The Bill and Melinda Gates Foundation is a legacy of the *Microsoft* success. Without the successful generation of the unprecedented market value that Microsoft has earned, the work of the Foundation could not be possible. *The Gates Foundation* has inspired many other billionaires to donate 50% of their wealth to philanthropic causes. It's a great example of how business can contribute to a healthy global community.

There are many examples of mixed sponsorship and philanthropic strategies that contribute to healthier communities. *Home Depot* participates in community programs with *Habitat for Humanity, Boys and Girls Clubs*, and provides grants to organizations across North America that incorporate sustainable building techniques and materials.

VanCity Savings Credit Union supports social enterprises through workplace and community diversity. They provide funds for strong business cases that create community learning and profitability. *VanCity* is a strong supporter for LGBT rights. In 1986 *VanCity* pioneered the first socially responsible mutual fund, called *Ethical Funds*. In recent years they introduced micro-lending to start up organizations for green businesses. *VanCity* were also founding partners of the *Sustainability Purchasing Network*, which promotes more responsible business practices.

A June 2007 article by Newman/Grigg outlined the psychological benefits where companies participate in either philanthropy or sponsorship programs. The three main benefits for staff were found in pride, meaning and purpose, and commitment. Successful philanthropic programs have identified the benefits of lower staff turnover, higher productivity, and better team performance.

The authors concluded that there is a greater psychological connection by staff to the cause when the form of giving has no strings attached. The annual *United Way* campaigns include organizations allowing staff to loan their time and talent in tangible support without there being a direct benefit to the organization. The article also said that employees recognize the difference between charitable activities and marketing schemes.

Supply management is involved in many charitable events with sponsorship programs leading to increased presence of corporate brands—especially in the public sector. The naming of public buildings and hospital facilities is not without considerable controversy. On one hand the sponsorship program may reduce the cost of school equipment paid from taxes while the catch may be an influence on the curriculum or be a part of a larger marketing campaign. A hospital may receive medical equipment with an expectation that its brand of supplies may be tied to the use of the equipment.

In September 2009, *Future Shop* (now *Best Buy)* sponsored a high school computer lab for the Toronto School Board. A part of this $100,000 agreement is that the labs be painted in the *Future Shop* corporate colors and that the schools are within 7 km of a *Future Shop*. In 2008, a Surrey, B.C. school board received $85,000 for a computer lab from *Future Shop*.

Since then, the Surrey School Board has strategically sought out corporate sponsorships through its business development department. It's sponsorship with *Chevron* and *MyClass Needs* has provided funds for 186 science-related projects. The Surrey School Board netted over $2 million dollars in fundraising and sponsorship activities in a one-year period. The Vancouver School Board when approached by *Chevron* says it was not set up to accept funds as a district but individual schools do participate. At issue is potential influence on curriculum content. For supply chain staff there can be a bias towards favoring products or services from sponsors and not necessarily having an open competition. It remains to be seen if this will be a growing trend to reduce the burden on taxpayers.

The Role for Consumer Responsibility

"Our personal consumer choices have ecological, social,
and spiritual consequences.
It is time to re-examine some of our deeply held notions
that underlie our lifestyles."
~ David Suzuki
Scientist, journalist and head of the Suzuki Foundation

Consumers are a divided group. Market forces tend to segment consumers into a variety of categories by metrics such as ethnicity, income, health, vocation, profession, geographical locations, age, taxpayer or not, and many other target groups. Marketing campaigns are strategically aimed at each target market with the aim of extracting as much money as is possible out of each consumer's pocket. If the pocket comes up short they will extend credit for almost anything that supports the seller's targeted interests. This may seem a little harsh but fundamentally it has been the role of business to maximize profits and maximizing revenues is but one of the tactics to doing so.

Consumers have been duped by misleading labels and many other questionable practices, which have led to a sense of consumptive entitlement. If one can afford it and it's for sale legally, then the consumer makes their personal choice based on their perceived need and ability to pay. The theory is that a consumer would never continue to consume until it adversely affected their health or financial well-being. Reality paints a different picture.

The cases of diabetes and other health issues and the effects of *super-sizing* fast foods have caused sellers to rethink their responsibilities and temper their enthusiasm for more and more sales. On the other hand, pharmaceutical companies can exploit this opportunity in the market where food purveyors have contributed to health problems.

On the subject of obesity, Dr. Richard L. Atkinson said, "Diet, exercise, and behavior modification just don't work in the long term. They require people to do unnatural things. The time has come to start thinking about drugs, when current treatment of obesity have failed." Unfortunately, Dr. Atkinson was a purported ghostwriter for pharmaceutical companies and supports a potentially dangerous trend in health. In short, you can't believe all you hear or read. It is particularly important to support the voices trying to get the truth to consumers when they are struggling against titans like pharmaceutical companies.

In 1998, Dr. Nancy Olivieri, a University of Toronto researcher, was ostracized by the Toronto Children's Hospital because she made public the health problems associated with her research related to a drug manufactured by *Apotex* to treat blood diseases in children. This threatened the Hospital's funding from *Apotex* for a research center. Olivieri turned much of her normally non-public research over to the public forum so consumers would know, and more investigations could be made.

Consumer action groups have been around for a long time. Boycotts of products are quite common. Faith-based consumer groups are also formed to address debatable moral issues. And, all of these civil action groups do make a difference, however, in terms of a global impact, only a small percentage of consumers make a conscious decision to support sustainable products and services.

Frito Lay was acknowledged for having designed one of the more innovative packaging products for its SunChips® brand in 2009. *Mintel*, the savvy market research company, bestowed the recognition on the *PepsiCo* business unit for the use of biodegradable PLA in chip bags.

The biodegradable PLA package was a first for the material and was hoped to be a product that demonstrated a strategy for more responsible packaging by the company. PLA would predictably compost within 4 months of disposal in contrast to multiple decades for conventional fossil fuel-based packaging.

However, a mounting protest by consumer complaints through social media about the high noise level created from the packaging has *Frito Lay* withdrawing the PLA design except for a few bagged products. However, in Canada, to counter the apparent boycott, the company has issued newspaper advertisements which state that SunChips® will continue to be sold in the PLA-designed bag.

If consumers continue to buy goods and services based strictly on economic benefits, without questioning the ethical or environmental implications, nothing will change. Degradation of the planet and human rights will continue while exploitive practices will be condoned by default.

Unfortunately, only a small percentage of investors seek socially responsible investments. Only a small percentage of North Americans choose public transit. Only a small percentage buy fair trade certified agricultural products, organic chocolate and vegetables, or are aware of how their meat products are raised. Only a small percentage consume tap water in refillable containers as opposed to buying bottled water. Only a small percentage will be concerned about the working conditions at the source of their clothing, and only a small percentage stop to consider how their electronic devices were brought to market. And so on.

Yet, optimistically, the small percentage is growing. Awareness is a large part of the change as informed consumers will make responsible choices when available, and responsible sellers will adapt their business model in response to consumer expectations. We have already seen changes in consumer purchasing in the retail clothing industry, as well as: an increase in the sale of organic products, the adoption of ILO standards, the implementation of municipal procurement policies based on more responsible practices, the growth of niche marketers to leverage the market opportunities for their corporate and community commitments, and, electric vehicles are appearing while *Hummers* are disappearing. Leading suppliers and brands have jumped on the green bandwagon by investing in alternative materials and energies as they pursue sustainable business models.

Consumers have a tremendous amount of *potential* to do good.
For the most part self-serving interests drive consumer behaviors and market interests. However, as awareness of affordable solutions and knowledge of how products and services are created and distributed, the more consumers will see their expectations of business behaviors align with their values. Being an informed consumer is not a passive exercise. To navigate your way through the plethora of information, be they misleading, fraudulent, or complex and accurate requires a lot of work. Issues are changing constantly as are the suppliers and products. *Going green is not easy!*

The history of hemp is a glimpse into the relationship between the consumer and the corporation. Hemp has been a valuable crop for thousands of years. Its seed oils were used for medicines and food while its fibers were used for clothing and ropes. Hemp was a farming crop in North America for about 250 years until the early 20th century.

During the period of prohibition in the US in the 1920s, hemp was banned as an intoxicant due to its association with marijuana and growing hemp became illegal. The cotton, forestry, and paper making industries lobbied in support of the ban on the competing hemp products, effectively preventing consumers from having access to this valuable source of material.

The sustainable attributes of hemp over other alternative crops is remarkable. Organic cotton requires 22,000 liters of water per kg of cotton lint while hemp only requires 2,200 liters. Bamboo requires a heavy chemical treatment to reduce its 25% binding lignin content while hemp contains 4% lignin. Most other textiles require a bleach bath to whiten while hemp requires a light peroxide rinse. Hemp stores large amounts of CO_2 while growing, is a hardy plant requiring little in pesticide or fertilization, and has a high commodity price.

In 1998, the cultivation and production of *industrial* hemp was permitted in Canada. Industrial hemp has only very small traces of the hallucinogenic drug TCP. It is not enough to get anyone "high". Hemp is returning to the clothing industry and food industry based on scientific research and not on "propaganda" from misleading sources with hidden agendas. Consumers again have access to this commercially viable and environmentally sustainable product that should never have been restricted from responsible producers.

Changing consumer behavior is a large part of the problem when trying to introduce energy efficient options. The smart metering and smart grid programs being introduced by companies like *B.C. Hydro* require consumers to want to conserve energy. The theory is that if consumers have data that tells them the cost of their electricity is cheaper at 1:00 a.m., they will run their washing machines at that time.

Families with piles of laundry generally are more likely motivated to keep on top of the task as opposed to the cost of electricity. Changing the pattern of behavior built on convenience and time availability in favor of saving a few dollars per year will be a challenge. The savings will have to be considerable to change the consumptive behavior.

Various studies peg Canadian water consumption per capita at 1600 cubic meters per year. Only the US exceeds Canada in water consumption. Further studies have shown that 1/3 of our residential drinking water is used to flush toilets. This shows us clearly that water has been taken for granted in Canada and undervalued as a resource. It takes informed and conscious consumers to insist on low-flow toilets and other water-conserving devices. They must be willing to not only change behaviors, but also see the past as wasteful and inefficient and the future as a correction of those ways.

The growth of the car-sharing business illustrates the willingness of consumers to make the adaptation in their behaviors. In 1994, the first car sharing non-profit cooperative was started in Montreal, *Communauto,* and stimulated the Vancouver car cooperative known as *Modo*. These car-sharing businesses keep more cars off the road while keeping rates competitive. *Modo* has a fleet of over 350 cars parked around Vancouver. Drivers only pay for their fair share of the use of a vehicle and pay no annual maintenance and insurance costs. *Car2Go*, one of its commercial competitors that offers one-way alternatives has 300+ vehicles in Vancouver and its customer membership is growing each

Larry Berglund

month. Also in Vancouver, the local *British Columbia Auto Association* has now added *Evo*, their car sharing for their members, leading the way for other auto associations. In Toronto, *AutoShare* and *Zipcar* have seen a rapid growth in the past four years. Whether the companies are nonprofit or for profit, automotive analyst Dave Zhao predicts 4.4 million car-share memberships in the market by 2016 with a fleet of 70,000 vehicles.

In Europe, it was *Daimler* that began offering a *Car2Go* service in 2009 (using its popular super compact *Smart* cars) and piloted the *Car2Go* program in North America. Electric vehicles are a popular choice for car-share drivers in many of the car-sharing organizations as most trips are local. However, the business opportunity is based on a willingness of consumers to change their behaviors and access affordable and responsible services, over the status of ownership.

The Who to the How

Now we understand who can make a difference in the endeavor to make sustainability a new global norm. It does touch all of us, in all of our roles, but for the average businessman, average manager and the average supply chain professional in any organization, whether for-profit, non-profit or a government institution, the question becomes less about who than how. The how may seem daunting, but after years of consulting with numerous companies and organizations, the process can be tackled in a logical way for those with the will to do it. Our next section on *How* will help anyone start that process and keep them on track.

How?

How?

Getting Started

Action expresses priorities.
~ Mohandas Gandhi

We've reached the most important part of the book: How to develop—and more importantly—implement an effective CSR strategy. If you are feeling overwhelmed at this point by the number of issues to take into consideration and who needs to get on board in order to effectively put these initiatives into practice, I completely understand. So let's take it one step at a time rather than getting over complicated.

Instead of a laundry list of things to do, I've chosen to categorize sustainability into four distinct categories. This gives an overall picture allowing you to effectively focus your CSR strategies for your particular company. It also gives you the scope to address sustainability on a number of fronts across a broad spectrum of issues.

Let's start with a definition:

Total cost of ownership (**TCO**) is a financial estimate intended to help buyers and sellers determine the direct and indirect **costs** of a product or system. It is a management accounting concept that can be used in full costs accounting or even ecological economics where it includes social costs.

Total cost of ownership requires that supply management take a pragmatic approach and prioritize those issues that you want to take on. You will find yourself being pulled in many directions by the various stakeholders that vow to save the planet at all costs to those who only buy the cheapest thing that's within their budget. One of the mantras to keep in mind when dealing with sustainability is to follow the money as each of these can be quantified and measured as a cost. There can be a lot of self-serving interests to wade through when trying to determine where you should spend your time and dollars to attain best value. Some marketers refer to this as the green bling, but keep in mind that cost within a sustainability context is a long, not a short-term, strategy.

The four quadrants to consider are: green products and services, socio/economic factors, emissions management, and resource conservation. Where you initiate your plan will depend on many factors and naturally will change from company to company, but this chart gives you a place to come back to and regularly check to determine if you are covering all bases.

The Four GREE(N) Quadrants

G R E E (N)

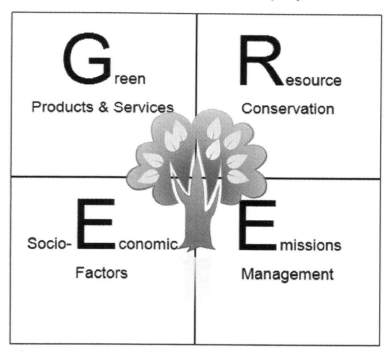

What's in The Four GREE(N) Quadrants:

Green products and services:

- √ Eliminate toxic materials
- √ Organics
- √ Sales and marketing focus
- √ Customer expectations
- √ Material substitution
- √ Material specifications
- √ Third party audits
- √ Technology
- √ International standards

Resource conservation:

- √ Reduce consumption of water and natural resource materials
- √ Assess alternative materials
- √ Food security
- √ Recycling programs
- √ LEED standards
- √ Lean manufacturing
- √ IT energy management
- √ Product life cycle

SocioEconomic factors:

- √ Protect workers' health and safety
- √ Engage with social enterprises
- √ Provide employment to disenfranchised people
- √ Philanthropy and sponsorship
- √ Local sourcing
- √ Living wage programs
- √ Fair trade programs
- √ Societal expectations
- √ Wage disparity
- √ Telecommuting

Emissions management:

- √ Reduce green house gases
- √ Alternative energy sources
- √ Biodiesel fuels
- √ Retrofitting buildings
- √ Responsible travel programs
- √ Fleet management/couriers
- √ Infrastructure energy management
- √ Carbon Offset strategies

Green Products and Services

Green products and services are the low hanging fruit where we find the quick wins for easily substituting toxic or non-renewable materials. Green products and services are generally produced in a sustainable manner. They are competitive, widely distributed and well-supported with 3rd party and international standards for consistent quality.

We previously mentioned that *Clorox* who teamed up with *The Sierra Club* to work on their green products, called Green Works™ created environmentally friendly cleaning products. These are products that your buyers need to be made aware of to give them as one of the green options all companies could be using for general cleaning done in their own office /warehouse/factory spaces. Or it could be a product that is specific to the industry you work in and part of your own manufacturing process. *Protocol Environmental Solutions* has formulated a unique line of InnerCrete™ Membrane Technology products for the mining industry.

The low hanging fruit of finding green products and services requires research and recommendations. It requires a certain amount of knowledge of what are real green products and what is referred to as greenwashing. Greenwashing is where there is language used in a product's description or labeling is designed to give the strong impression it is a sustainable or socially conscious or fair trade product when it is absolutely not. If your supply chain managers are staying current with these issues, then choosing green products and services should be on everyone's list.

However, depending on what your company or organization is doing it may make very little environmental impact. You can use green cleaning products in the office, but if you are wasting paper by the ton your office can make a greater environmental impact through Resource Conservation.

 Resource Conservation

Resource conservation involves reducing consumption of water and natural resource materials. For builders or building projects it would mean understanding LEED standards (Leadership in Energy and Environmental Design). For buyers and other supply chain managers it would mean assessing alternative materials. For operations people it will mean understanding a product life cycle and the recycling programs that you may need to initiate, like reclaiming the mercury in compact fluorescent lights previously mentioned. It means creating efficiency using principles such as lean manufacturing. It also means ensuring that no product creation practices will interfere with food crops that ensure sustainability in whatever country you are operating in or contracting with. A previous example being that corn ethanol may interfere with food sustainability, which brings us to socioeconomic factors.

 Socioeconomic Factors

These are the factors that are, at bottom line, global human rights issues where exploitation is disallowed or made illegal. True CSR moves towards a win-win for workers, their communities, and the organizations that employ them. These include the protection of workers' health and safety, addressing wage disparities, fair trade programs, fair hiring practices, etc. All would have shared their success at connecting the 3Es:

1. Economic interests
2. Environmental responsibilities
3. Expectations of society

Sweatshop awareness gained notoriety in the mid 90s when high profile branding companies such as the *GAP* and *Kathie Lee Gifford's* clothing line were revealed to be sourcing their production in conditions which contravened International Labour Organization conventions and other human rights issues. Further revelations were found with *Disney* and *Mattel*, to be followed by investigations in the supply chains of *Nike, Adidas, Reebok, Umbro, Mire, and Brine.*

The public, when made aware, have communicated their intolerance of exploitive practices that have gone on for years. In a landmark example, the one hundred year old *Russell Clothing*, now a subsidiary of *Fruit of the Loom* brand, was successfully boycotted by many U.S., British, and Canadian university and college students. The students worked with the Worker Rights Consortium to organize the boycott against Russell. At issue was the labor relations fiasco in Russell's factory in the Honduras, which had been closed for 10 months, allegedly to prevent its 1200 workers from participating in union/organization activities. In November 2009, the company conceded defeat and agreed to reopen the factory along with wage increases and reinstated union rights. The message was heard by other brand managers such as *Levi Strauss* operating in Haiti and *Knights Apparel* in the Dominican Republic who were threatening similar actions against their workers, but retracted their threats.

A look at the *Fiji Water Company's* (FWC) operation points out some of the issues related to CO_2 emissions and health. The FWC draws water from a spring in Fiji, bottles it, and ships it as far as 10,000 miles to discriminating consumers in Great Britain. According to a BBC documentary, 1/3 of Fijians don't have access to safe drinking water. Local typhoid problems have been linked to contaminated water. While the export of water has been a boon to the economy, FWC needs to do more work on all of the 3Es. If there were a tax on the emissions of the imported water in Britain it would make sense. Drinking water in Britain is readily available from a tap which is low cost, does not increase emissions and keep Fiji's water in Fiji where it is needed for the health of their own communities. Now, someone needs to figure out how to add economic value to Fiji without it creating an environmental and health cost that is unacceptable.

Being a CSR organization means not just being forced to choose people and environment over profits, but to actively find the balance that works for everyone. Like *Mountain Equipment Co-op* that routinely inspects its factories in China, imposes their own standards, and helps their contractors become in compliance, moving away from exploitive or unhealthy practices.

 ## Emissions Management

Emissions Management is probably the area in the four quadrants that will make the deepest impact on the environmental crisis our planet is now facing. Therefore, when planning and prioritizing, I recommend all companies find a way to reduce their contributions on green house gas (GHG) emissions. Can alternative fuels be used that reduce or have no impact? Can buildings be retrofitted and solar energy exploited? Do you have telecommuting and responsible travel programs including fleet and courier management? All infrastructure should be analyzed for where greater reductions in emissions, or efficient energy use can be created. And, at last resource, can your company support carbon offsetting projects? Offsetting projects like planting trees, supporting nonprofits like SELF, the *Solar Electric Light Fund* that help third world communities that burn coal and firewood, to now have a solar energy system that will last them years with little or no negative environmental impact. Offsetting projects can help the global impact be reduced, but should be explored only after your own house is in order.

 ## What it Takes

In each of the four quadrants it is up to the supply management team to be responsible for:

- **Leadership:** Gaining Stakeholder Buy-in, Creating a Value Proposition, Assigning Research
- **Capacity Building:** Staff Training, Communication and Compliance
- **Budget and Business:** Cost Management, Risk Management
- **Staying Current:** Research, Monitoring and Reporting Activities

Already this may seem challenging to you to take on, so I will outline some recommended steps and suggest how to create priorities that are customized to your own environment, whether it be a government department, a retail outlet, or a manufacturing operation. In each of the following sections we will move from a general outline to specific details to keep in mind and put into action.

Developing a Plan for Sustainability

7 Stages

The following are brief summary outline of stages that I recommend any organization can use to get started. Beyond these descriptions, we will go into greater details of each of the following seven stages.

Seven Stages Towards Implementation

1. Leadership—Create a Team that Creates Philosophies and Policies

This step involves creating leadership as well as involving the stakeholders of your CSR strategy. In larger organizations it is easier to have a smaller team that spearheads, researches, makes recommendations and communicates it to get agreement and buy-in from all levels. This is the team that will create the outline for policies or philosophies and determine what the core values are that the organization wants to reflect in your CSR projects.

2. Prioritize and Plan

Using the GREE(n) quadrants, figure out the areas that your own organization fits and where you are going to make the most social or environmental impact. To analyze this you may need the help of a consultant or third party organization and I will discuss this further. You can also use the Resources section in the back of this book.

Your aim in this stage is to create a list of projects and add timelines for CSR strategies to be put in place for each one. Each project may be a long-term process or a short-term process. The most complicated changes may be several years down the road, but at least there will be a plan for these changes.

3. Budget and Business Case

Taking a total cost of ownership approach and by prioritizing where you can align your supply chain needs with your corporate objectives, you can begin to see where resources are required. The business case needs to be objective and ensure that if the actions are successful, it will provide a meaningful commitment to meet CSR and stakeholder expectations. Start with the low hanging fruit – low risk. But also lower returns. Don't stop at the low hanging fruit. You will be able to realize savings with an appropriate strategy under the Green products and services quadrant. Use these savings to develop a self-financing model to support your CSR initiatives. If the organization can see that supply chain practices in CSR are adding value and not costs, it creates support for more actions to take place.

While out-of-pocket costs are easier to predict you may need some assistance on more subjective cost savings. What might it save your organization if it reduced staff turnover due to its engaging CSR strategy, for example?

Don't lose sight of the bottom line. Be pragmatic and achieve results that give short term and long-term financial benefits in addition to feel good accomplishments. Who do you have on your leadership team who can analyze, watch and balance this?

4. Working with Social Entities

Your aim is to not only find the ideal social entity partners that your organization should be teaming, but to nurture a learning relationship. You need to know what they know and what the deeper concerns are.

Social entities or social entrepreneurs are in every community. They can assist in finding local staffing resources, materials and resources, and provide meaningful work to those less fortunate. Your company can work with social entities and contract for a percentage of goods and services that will have direct benefits and redistribute the revenues in your neighborhoods.

Social entities are often not-for-profit organizations which run just like other business models—based on a strong mission statement and sense of purpose—not necessarily to generate profits in order to function.

5. Communication and Training

Have a communication strategy. The people on the front line need to know that they are a big part of the transition; so make sure you let everyone—both internal and external stakeholders—know. This involves creating online information updates, sharing the credit, developing sourcing guides for better choices, developing a resource of reference materials, and using web-based training to reduce costs of maintaining the programs. Everyone needs to know that their actions are making a difference.

6. Working with Your Suppliers

You can't be CSR compliant without holding all your suppliers to a standard of compliance. How do you do this and maintain your business relationships and your financial advantages? We will look at this in more detail later.

7. Staying Current

A best practice today can be a common practice tomorrow. Don't be satisfied with the status quo. Continue to develop and promote leading practices. Make sustainable practices a core value in the DNA of your business and attend conferences to stay current. There should be passionate people on your team that love to research. These are people who will go to conferences and keep their fingers on the pulse. And return to act!

 # Expanding on the Seven Stages

None of the below stages come without challenges. We will try to guide you in more specific advice and troubleshooting. Also, as much as we have laid it out as steps, this is rarely how it happens. You can start implementation, especially in small things immediately, but for a successful strategy you will want to follow these stages and return to them as needed.

 # Stage #1 - Leadership

Create a Team that Creates Philosophies and Policies

Buy-in from senior management is essential. They need to be willing to support a formal team to bring CSR onboard. It will be the team itself that does the research and delivers it to the stakeholders. Yet, the senior management's concerns must be addressed, and so that they can feel fully on board and the team can do its research for them.

Here are some prompts for the executives I have worked with which they have found helpful:

1. What types of market intelligence have you gathered with respect to your organization's products/services from a CSR perspective?
2. Which types of information are you concerned with being exposed about your company? Why?
3. Which resources are you consuming that could be conserved through changes in your practices or processes?
4. How do your customers deal with non-value added costs associated with your products or services?
5. What is the buzz about your business from staff, peers, and others?
6. What do your key stakeholders think about CSR?
7. Where might you be exposed to liabilities within the next 3-5 years?
8. What is changing your industry?
9. Where can you demonstrate leadership or differentiate your company in the market from a CSR perspective?
10. What are you doing now to demonstrate CSR to your stakeholders?
11. What if you do nothing?

The questions above reflect external and internal interests alongside risk management and preemptive strategies. They reiterate the need for continuously defining values in your upstream and downstream supply management decisions.

The leadership needs to share their answers to these questions with a designated team. If you are spearheading the CSR project you can start creating that team by identifying the CSR champions within the organization on the horizontal and vertical axes. There will be many – especially in the younger generation. A typical team could have these critical company stakeholders:

- Member or members of the executive / company leadership
- The senior members of supply chain management
- Entry and mid-level members of supply chain staff who are eager advocates of CSR
- Marketing, public relations or communications department representative
- Operations management representative
- Accounting or financial expertise
- Major supplier representative
- Human resources representative
- Non-governmental organization representative
- External advisor with CSR expertise

Your team may have more or less people. They may come together or share virtually as a whole to report what a sub group project has accomplished.

The Executives that will be on the team, and therefore be responsible for it to the other members of the executive, must have a sense that their communication needs to reflect consistency. The organization's audio and video must match. They must walk the talk. People tend to believe what they hear and see leaders do. The *Herman Miller* organization has long been recognized for its leadership in designing office furnishings that are aimed at eliminating waste and conserving natural resources. This is a strategic direction set by their CEO Brian Walker, an advocate for *doing the right thing*. Their goals for 2020 include no landfill waste, no hazardous waste, no air/water emissions from manufacturing, and 100% green energy.

Once you have your team, the next stage will be working with your team on the three primary tasks:

1. Creating the Organizations written Core Values in regard to CSR
2. Creating an Ethical Purchasing Policy
3. Creating a companion Code of Conduct Policy for your suppliers

Policies are only as good as the people behind them, so make sure that you first agree on your company's core values in regards to CSR.

Core Values Statements for CSR

In order to discuss Core Values Statements and other foundation documents, I am going to use the benchmark of *Patagonia*.

Here is an excerpt of *Patagonia's* Core Values:

For us at Patagonia, *a love of wild and beautiful places demands participation in the fight to save them, and to help reverse the steep decline in the overall environmental health of our planet. We donate our time, services and at least 1% of our sales to hundreds of grassroots environmental groups all over the world who work to help preverse the tide.*

We know that our business activity – from lighting stores to dyeing shirts – creates pollution as a by-product. So we work steadily to reduce those harms. We use recycled polyester in many of our clothes and only organic, rather than pesticide-intensive, cotton.

Staying true to our core values during thirty plus years in business has helped us create a company we're proud to run and work for. And our focus on making the best products possible has brought us success in the marketplace.

When moving forward to write all other policies that will govern future behaviors and training, this statement can be used as a compass for anyone and everyone in the company. For some guidance on how to get to your core values statement, we recommend you use an outside facilitator with your team. Facilitators have a bag of techniques and games that help achieve consensus and rank priorities.

After stating the values of the company and agreeing on their adoption, the next task is to draft a procurement policy that also meets the approval of the senior executive. The policy should articulate the organization's business philosophy and the scope of the CSR core values statement. In tandem, you can also work on developing a companion code of conduct for your organization's suppliers. The Internet access to policies written by leading organizations makes this step much easier now.

Ethical Purchasing Policies & Supplier Codes of Conduct

Canada, Europe and the US now require private and public sector organizations to adopt Ethical Purchasing Policies (EPPs) along with supplier codes of conduct. The cities of Vancouver, B.C. and Los Angeles, California were among the first North American municipalities to adopt EPPs. The Canadian university book stores have been active in ensuring their branded clothing and novelty items are meeting ILO standards to comply with both their EPP and their respective supplier codes of conduct.

The issue of monitoring supplier performance for compliance is a key part of these programs.

Most of the brand management companies adopted various forms of EPPs along with supplier codes of conduct. Supplier codes of conduct generally reference the ILO standards at a minimum, along with other corporate values. By way of example, in 1997 *Mattel* developed a set of Global Manufacturing Principles which sets the human rights, health and safety, environmental, cultural and ethnic, and philosophical standards which must be complied to by suppliers, subcontractors and licensees and others that do business with Mattel.

Mattel has the independent monitoring organization, International Center for Corporate Accountability, to report out on their progress regularly. Monitoring production conditions across the supply chain is a very challenging commitment, given the distance and diversity of issues to be faced.

Child labor is a zero tolerance issue, said *Mattel*. Yet, in spite of *Mattel's* eight year's of experience in 2005 the *NY Times* reported allegations of child labor, verbal abuse, forced overtime, making workers buy special tool belts they could barely afford and restricting freedom of association. The offending supplier was domestic, *Rubies Costume Co.* in Richmond Hill, N.Y., but operating in Mexico.

Mattel requires employees to be at least 16 years old. *Rubies* acknowledged an audit by *Mattel* turned up one 15-year-old yet Mexican law allows 14-15 year olds to work a reduced day. *Rubies,* as a result of the *Mattel* audit, have promised to hire employees older than 16 years old and to correctly pay overtime. One employee claims the *Rubies'* plant manager altered her birth certificate and hired her at 14 years of age. This slip up underlines the need to monitor all supplier performance vigilantly.

Once these allegations are reported it is difficult for organizations to erase the negative stain. To *Mattel's* credit, they would appear to be doing as much as possible to stem problems within their supply chain to meet their corporate commitments. Your team needs to decide how they can be sure that their suppliers are not covering up injustices and fudging audits. Even *Enron* had an ethical code of conduct yet what makes an effective supplier code of conduct is clarity of wording and monitoring for compliance. In my opinion, one of the best is from *Patagonia*.

Not only is *Patagonia's* Supplier Workplace Code of Conduct clear and concise, they back it with a thirty-three page compliance benchmark when assessing supplier performance. *Patagonia's* Code is four pages in length and covers all of the relevant issues from legal obligations to quality management.

Given the economic, environmental and social performance of *Patagonia*, it would appear that they know how to walk the talk. With one of the highest staff retention rates in the retail industry, *Patagonia's* values resonate with their staff and high customer loyalty.

VanCity Savings Credit Union's purchasing group evaluates the *community leadership* that is demonstrated to staff and community by their suppliers. Financial Institutions may be inherently conservative and frugal but they also recognize that value goes beyond price.

Remember, policies are the means and not the end. Avoid being passive and be professional with the consistent implementation of the policy. It will mean changing behaviors, which is one of the biggest barriers to overcome and why buy-in from leadership is essential. If there is resistance to buying in, review the 9 Reasons for CSR again.

Learning Outcomes for Leaders

- Supply professionals should try to forecast the long-term effects of increased energy prices on the cost of goods and services
- Budget processes should encourage incentives for smart energy
- Procurement policies should include sustainability strategies
- The total life cycle costs of products should be factored into final decisions
- Procurement policies need to be effective and responsive during all economic conditions
- Supply professionals need to dialogue with strategic supplier initiatives to see ahead of the curve
- Outsourcing and off shoring economic models need to include energy and emission costs
- Outsourcing and off shoring may have run their course as cost cutting strategies – where will the new regional suppliers be found?
- Local sourcing strategies should be revisited to ensure their effectiveness
- Local sourcing shouldn't be an either/or proposition

Motorola embraced the benefits of quality management principles decades ago. Jack Welch while at *GE* adopted the *Motorola* quality program to increase profitability. *Toyota* integrated quality with relentless manufacturing efficiencies to differentiate its products in a crowded market and designed the highly successful *Prius*. Today, CSR is a duty to be performed by business executives for societies because it contributes to a more responsible business model with profitability as one of the outcomes.

Leadership demonstrated through CSR activities is being accepted by more corporate leadership in every market. Leaders recognize that a CSR strategy is a progressive means of achieving results that are measured in the long-term. It takes many small steps to get there. And the "there" is changing as more awareness of practices, policies, and products are demonstrated in the market. The more successes that CSR leaders can share, the more likely it is that CSR will continue to be an integral part of defining the success of a business and its leadership.

 ## Stage #2 - Prioritize and Planning

Using the Four Quadrants you should be able to begin your own prioritizing and planning of projects, whether it starts at the low-hanging fruit of Green Products and Services, or starts at the greatest impact in Emissions Management, or you want to create a full Four Quadrant Impact towards a CSR strategy. You will want to read the rest of this book, but your aim will be to make a list of all possible projects (you don't have to do them all, or all at once), and estimate roughly how quickly each can be researched and implemented.

In your research process, which will include business case analysis and communication with stakeholders and other partners, you will naturally come to the task of creating attainable milestones for each project. Again, you can rely on the help of CSR consultants, but it is the agreed upon priorities, budget limits and business cases that will be the major factor to creating meaningful and realistic milestones.

Set goals and targets. Measure your progress along the way. Once you get the initiative rolling you can correct your aim as you proceed for better results. What will your strategy look like in 3-5 years? How will you conduct the market intelligence to prepare for revised targets? Measures can include objective and subjective assessments—both may be equally as important. For example, target 25% of your contracts for services within 3 years to include labor from social entities – objective. Target improved customer satisfaction by providing greener choices in the products you sell – subjective.

If time and internal assets are not available consider external outsourcing CSR expertise. Work with industry or professional associations and participate in CSR buying networks like *Buy Social Canada.* The access to information is not the issue – it is the appropriate filtering of the information to find what you can adopt or adapt reasonably quickly. CSR will not be successful as a 'side job' on a to-do list for current staff that are trying to address day-to-day operational concerns. Now, its time to bring this to leadership and really create a team that will be successful.

Stage #3 - Budgeting and Business Case

In organizations, nothing goes forward without a budget or business case, but we have to look at this in a new way. Here is an easy example of how spending more can save money when being more responsible:

Costs	Device A	Device B	Device C
Acquisition	$1500 35%	$900 26%	$875 24%
Acquisition Process	$150 4%	$150 4%	$150 4%
5-year Consumables	$1800 42%	$1700 49%	$2400 65%
Support	$700 16%	$630 18%	$160 4%
Disposal	$100 2%	$100 3%	$100 3%
5-year TCO	$4250	$3380	$3685

The lowest out-of-pocket cost is Device C, which is only $875.00 but still costs 10% more than the best *TCO valued* Device B (lowest TCO $3380). If a department manager was given authority to buy a new office copier with a budget of $1500.00, the organization could end up with Device A which meets the budget expense, but will cost an additional $870.00 over Device B which has the best TCO value!

The budget process should take a total cost of ownership approach and allocate the funds accordingly. This means the capital and operating budgets need to reflect total costs should not be seen as independent resources, rather as pooled resources, to attain the best value over the long-term.

The business case for electric and hybrid vehicles creates a dilemma when trying to choose between market options. A hybrid car may cost $30,000 and only cost $.15 per mile to operate; while a conventional car costs $15,000 and $.30 per mile to operate. However, a driver would need to put on 100,000 miles before reaching the break-even point, based on the total cost of ownership. Economics sustainability does matter at some point.

Green Business Loans

When budgeting your CSR transformation you may want to consider a Green Business Loan. *The VanCity Savings Credit Union* provides loans to businesses, not-for-profits, housing co-ops, and property-managed strata groups to buy energy efficient heating systems or boilers to save energy. They provide grants towards community-based initiatives that support climate change programs. *VanCity* provides loans to purchase fuel-efficient vehicles at preferred rates to encourage the reduction of the carbon footprint. These savings provide a self-funded payback program. Is there a credit union or a bank in your area that you can use for your greening projects?

When beginning this journey consider new approaches when looking for solutions. Total cost of ownership models based on objective business cases will assist with prioritizing your efforts. Learn to walk before you run.

Small and medium enterprises (SMEs) are a large part of our economies. As global players they are also gaining a presence through the micro credit programs that are being established. The operation of non-profit banking institutions such as the *Grameen Bank* is taking effect. The *Grameen Bank,* founded by Nobel Prize recipient Muhammad Yunus, is an example of the new entrepreneurs who have not had access to credit in the past, now being able to create a successful business.

Supply professionals may need to be sourcing products and services from this new generation of entrepreneurs that don't have the credit ratings we are used to reviewing for risk assessment. We may have to develop new selection criteria to encourage SMEs domestically and internationally in order to attain innovative or competitively priced goods. This awareness of how supply chains affect the distribution of wealth has been understood when we consider the multiplier effect within the automotive industry or high tech sectors, that is, the way benefits and money ripple outward. It is less understood within the emerging economies as to how SMEs play a role is supplying Western consumers and commercial interests.

One way to budget is to use a life cycle cost analysis (LCC) or total cost of ownership (TCO). These can be very complex and require engineering studies using probabilistic and deterministic valuations along with other calculations. These calculations include the initial asset cost and future discounted expenses, along with forecasts of the cost of maintenance operating and repairs, plus the cost of disposal by the end user. The point of all of this is, to go beyond the usual out of pocket cost projections for a 1-2 year period (ex: how it effects other resources and line items in the future), and use all your data in a practical and unbiased way.

Payback models that account for the risk hurdles are simpler versions of life cycle cost analyses (LCC), which most business people are familiar with. Payback models look at how various decisions will influence future revenues, cash flows or energy savings, and are quite intuitive in nature. Adding emissions, or other incremental measures is not that complex and can lead to a better-informed decision.

The most important thing is to get someone on your team who is the budgeting and financial whizz who will be able to understand and work with these concepts in order to help your team determine which projects will have what kind of payback when. Note that some of these paybacks will be beyond monetary returns with the idea that everything will be taken into account, literally.

 ## Stage #4 - Communication and Training

Communication is the key to most successful implementations so we will look at all your communication from suppliers, to third party audit organizations and social entities, so you have some ideas of how you can communicate with them. It is, however, your communication and training with your staff that will remain the most critical.

It cannot be stated strongly enough that staff training is essential for CSR success. This means that not only is it important to create awareness and understanding amongst the supply management staff but it is essential that this also be communicated with all other staff for there to be a sense of pride and ownership. The integration of organizational values with marketing operational practices, design, finance and sourcing strategies must be consistent. The reporting across the organization should reflect its core values with respect to CSR.

Everyone needs to be onboard and you will want to work with training and HR departments, or hire appropriate consultants to design effective training. On your own you can develop staff forums and brain storming sessions. How will you communicate successes, reward positive behaviors, instill pride and celebrate your accomplishments?

Beyond the staff, you must right away engage with other stakeholders such as current suppliers. Many of your suppliers may have demonstrated a working knowledge of CSR practices. Start to engage with NGOs, and contact community agencies and social entrepreneurs. Gather the issues of interest and concern that will need to be addressed in a policy. The subject matter is evolving on business fronts and on political agendas. The CSR champions will be conduits for ideas internally and externally.

Forums with Stakeholders

You will be happy to know that governments at all levels in North America practice forums with stakeholders on CSR issues. While I was with the City of Vancouver we held forums of this type. How much is for show and how much is the 8th sin of greenwashing, lip service, depends again on the executive buy-in and leadership. Yet, there are exemplar companies who have made these conferences all about CSR.

One such company which successfully holds stakeholder forums is *Unilever*. In 2007, it established the internationally recognized Responsible Sourcing Policy sponsored by the European Brands Association (called AIM), and the Grocery Manufacturing Association in North America. *Unilever's* forum invites over 35 consumer goods producers *and* their suppliers to discuss the means of supporting responsible sourcing and production. These companies' decisions affect millions of consumers.

On a smaller scale, local companies can invite their key suppliers and NGOs to annual forums to discuss emerging issues and best practices. In essence, the forums leverage the collective knowledge in the market to advance responsible sourcing which benefits the entire market. This market knowledge helps a company to be more competitive.

What commonly happens is, the major players in the market share ideas for driving efficiencies and gathering information on supply chain social compliance performance. When they find best practices in these areas, the information is relayed between the participating companies and helps to change standards across the globe.

So why not be proactive and hold in-house forums inviting stakeholders to provide their input and to share your organization's commitments to CSR and sustainability. Yes this can be intimidating but it can also lead to meaningful dialogues on market opportunities and decrease your risks. Discerning consumers will play a stronger role affecting business models in the future as awareness of responsible options increases.

Sharing of Information

A hallmark of leading organizations is the willingness to share their success and failures with sustainability initiatives. As CSR and sustainability is a largely voluntary process this is a critical component to advancing the sustainability agenda. Supply professionals have many avenues to engage in dialogue on the practices and problems that exist. Business associations provide the means through forums and conferences for discussion. Newsletters and business publications are other mediums to share ideas. Another proactive way for professionals to participate in drafting the mandate for CSR is through networks.

Supply management should be the internal resource and external communication contact to coordinate sustainability initiatives involving the acquisition of goods services and equipment. There should be links to the supply management web site to ethical suppliers under contract, links to green products and services, principles and codes of conduct as well as current initiatives and contact names for more information should be readily available.

The next generation, who will take over the leadership in business and politics, will, in time, share views on a global communication network that will ferret out unacceptable practices. It is already happening. The likelihood of being exposed if you have unethical practices is far greater. Once these allegations are reported it is difficult for organizations to respond effectively without inviting further criticism. But, those businesses that connect the 3Es (Environment responsibility, Economic interests and Expectations of the Community), will continue to reap the rewards.

Celebrating Successes

Have fun. Share success stories and reward achievements. Share the experiences with colleagues outside your business. Inside, hold local food days and create fun games. Perkins+Will's Vancouver office has a *Pass the Trash* competition that recognizes the office with the highest diversion rate and the Perkins+Will *Energy Cup* competition, which is a unique online competition that pits virtual office race cars against one another, the more power saved the further the race car travels.

At *BMO Financial Group*, over 100 employees act as in-house *Environmental Ambassadors* and work to raise awareness of environmental issues and champion the bank's sustainability strategies, including the formal *ECO Strategy* that addresses its energy consumption, transportation, material consumption, waste management and procurement policies.

At *Lush Handmade Soaps* they call their in-house sustainability positions *Eco Warriors* and at the Vancouver and Toronto locations manage their own community gardens to grow an assortment of fruits and vegetables throughout the year—complete with rainwater harvesting systems, composting, mason bees and hummingbird feeders.

Xerox uses Earth Day to acknowledge and get more people involved in sustainable programs. This includes e-waste collection drives and free home energy audits. *Microsoft* holds e-waste collection days on their campuses. *HP* offers free bike tune-ups and lunch presentations on energy efficient vehicles. *Symantec* hosts vendor fairs to present energy saving ideas and equipment. *Timberland* sponsors community events and invites its vendors to participate with them. *Sun Microsystems* enabled their staff to measure their personal environmental footprint.

Many organizations have local food days with products from local farms. Forming green teams helps to monitor commitments and find other projects to initiate. Through intranet sites staff can be recognized as a team member (greenies) or for their individual achievements towards CSR goals. While prizes can help with the recognitions by individuals or groups, having the commitments acknowledged by senior management is really important. This in turn inspires more ideas.

 ## Stage #5 - Working with Social Entities

Most business associations have members from the nonprofit sector, which includes social entities or social entrepreneurs. These organizations create meaningful employment to the underemployed in your community. SEs ensure safe working environments, competitive wage rates, and often times assist with social services for the people they employ. Supply chain managers can allocate a percentage of goods and/or services to be sourced from SEs. *Buy Social* is a very active network that contributes to the connections between business and SEs to serve society better.

Philanthropy, Sponsorships, and Business

We have already mentioned partnerships in Philanthropy (Foundations) or Sponsorships (*Future Shop*, now *Best Buy*, sponsoring school computer labs) or even Social enterprises (*Newman's Own*) or enterprises that have a social purpose (*Stonyfield Farms*).

The questions is when, who and how should you seek out a partnership?

When should happen when you think your organization has capacity, meaning the will and the resources to make a strong CSR company that can take the next step. It means the leadership of your company is firmly on board.

Who to partnership with depends on your own Code of Ethics and mission. Whatever your organization wants to do to make a difference you can usually find partners that can help you, or provide mutual benefits. Your research team should look into what is being done out there already. One way is to talk to your industry associations to see if others have been seeking partnerships. Associations are often approached before businesses or have programs already.

If you are an entrepreneur, you could also consider creating a social enterprise rather than a pure, for-profit organization. One of the best examples of social entrepreneurs is *Newman's Own Inc*. Founded by the late Paul Newman in 1982, it combines philanthropic interests, societal benefit programs and healthy food products as well as pet foods. *Newman's Own* was years ahead of its time in terms of socio/economic involvement.

Supply professionals can work with local social entrepreneurs such as H.A.V.E. In Vancouver H.A.V.E. provides culinary training services to disenfranchised people. This provides a connection to not-for-profit social programs and addresses staffing resource shortages and training for local businesses. H.A.V.E. is operated by a local businessman who has made a personal commitment to the downtown east side of Vancouver. Most communities have social entrepreneurs and social enterprises to engage with local established businesses. These are *not* government-funded programs. Social entrepreneurs are replacing the charity-based models where the latter is aimed at helping the needy and the former is giving people dignified employment which builds communities.

Do social enterprises like H.A.V.E. make a difference? Here is a story from Laura Hayes working on a H.A.V.E. project through the B.C. Restaurant & Food Services Association.

"Jackie is a survivor of the residential schools that displaced and abused thousands of Aboriginal children from 1920–1996. Jackie has spent three years of her life down and out, drug addicted and having lost everything to the streets of the downtown eastside. Two years ago Jackie found herself at a job fair at the corner of Hastings and Main and it was here that she met Chef Glen an instructor from the H.A.V.E Cafe Culinary Training Center. Jackie enrolled in the eight-week culinary training course and after working with the instructors and the onsite career counselor at H.A.V.E. Jackie is now happily employed in a restaurant kitchen working alongside Chef Brian Fowke, one of Vancouver's most notable chefs."

When asked what H.A.V.E meant to her Jackie replies, "It changed my life". She credits H.A.V.E with boosting her self confidence and teaching her valuable job skills and assisting her in obtaining the position working with Chef Fowke. Jackie is truly an inspiration.

Starworks Packaging in Vancouver is a social entrepreneur that has successfully brought people with disabilities together and provides them with meaningful work in the community. Their customers are private and public sector organizations. *Starworks* continues to expand its operations and provide meaningful working opportunities to people that can be marginalized in society. *Starworks* can only be successful if businesses see value in the services which are offered. Given the growth of *Starworks* their future looks bright.

Mission Possible through its Executive Director Brian Postelwait has done a remarkable job of finding meaningful employment within the downtown east side of Vancouver for many people with employment barriers. For two decades the faith-based *Mission Possible* has reached out to public and private sector organizations to provide services and contribute to the economic and social development of this ravaged municipal sector. As a social entrepreneur, *Mission Possible* is another great example of seeing past the social problems and creating value where none existed.

The nonprofit organization *Canadian Aboriginal and Minority Supplier Council* (CAMSC) was formed in Canada a few years ago. Its mandate is to increase economic development and employment with small medium enterprises. The member companies that sponsor CAMSC are generally larger corporations with U.S and Canadian operations. CAMSC partners with the US-based National Minority Supplier Development Council Inc.

Habitat for Humanity (HFH), a not-for-profit, faith-based organization has a mission to provide affordable housing to break the cycle of poverty noticed the opportunity to accept used building materials that can be resold through their ReStore outlets. More commercial buildings were being converted to LEED standards so commercial property owners invite HFH into the buildings and offices that are slated for retrofitting to choose salvageable materials. HFH take the items and resell them back to the market. Used carpet tiles as one item which would normally end up in a landfill have been rescued and recycled for a longer life. Businesses can partner with HFH in their communities to expand the recycling of materials.

Socioeconomic benefits result from these types of community partnerships that are largely based on voluntary agreements.

 ## Stage #6 - Working with Your Suppliers

The first step in working with your suppliers is clarity and that will need to start with your Supplier Code of Conduct. Although CSR and sustainability are based on voluntary codes, as is a supplier code of conduct, there is an important legal note for supply professionals. You need to make the code a part of the terms and conditions in a contract. This makes the code a legally binding contractual commitment which must be complied with during the performance of the agreement. Failure to comply could lead to a breach of contract by the supplier. As much as voluntary codes appear benign, we can make them more effective when executing agreements.

Where there is a failure of a supplier to meet some of the conditions of a supplier code of conduct, this does not mean that you cannot work with that supplier. If the supplier can demonstrate a willingness to improve their ethical performance within an acceptable time frame, this helps to raise the bar. Evidence of a continuing effort to meet a supplier code of conduct speaks to the value that voluntary codes can achieve.

A supplier code of conduct sets the expectations for an ethical performance from a supplier. It is not intended to be a punitive statement. So don't write it so it sounds like it is. It is intended to provide clear direction on how it will affect business practices and relationships. A supplier code of conduct is not a stand alone document per se; it complements the strategic organizational goals.

The sustainability principles embedded in policy can take a couple of forms. There can be a *prescriptive model* which is narrow in scope and is directed at targeted goods or services. For example, the City of Vancouver took this approach with its policy aimed at fair trade certified agricultural products and clothing and uniforms. Their scope was intentional as this was an approach taken by an early adopter that wanted to deliver on political pledges. Therefore, it was kept within a reasonable scope to be successful and to learn from this first phase.

Another statement of sustainability principles for supply management can be based on a *principled model*. This implies that the scope is much broader and is intended to be inherent in all supply decisions. It also provides latitude for managerial judgment in its application. It is recommended that the responsibility for the supplier code of conduct rest with a senior manager or at a director level.

Of note is the use of a *complaint-based process* to handle complaints laid against a supplier. Essentially a complaint-based process requires the buyer's organization to investigate bona fide complaints and to take remedial action where necessary. The purpose is to ensure that unsubstantiated complaints laid by a single party do not cause the buyer's organization to enter into a protracted process which would have little effect. Whereas, if there were complaints brought about by registered NGOs and this was found to be corroborated in the public domain through other references, there would be an expectation that appropriate follow up action would be taken by senior management. A subsequent report would be filed against this supplier with respect to remedial actions.

One of the common debates on CSR arises as to how the buyer's organization can monitor a supplier's conduct in a foreign country. The cost to travel would be one concern but also the technical skills that could be required to determine as to whether the infractions are apparent or real.

Presuming that a legitimate complaint was provided to the buyer organization, the buyer's could require a sustainability audit report from a third party audit organization, such as *AsiaInspection*. Based on this information, an appropriate action could be determined. The noncompliance issue of using forced or child labor is usually subject to the termination of a contract. Based on the due diligence up front in the process the probability of complaints is very low.

Where infractions are found to be legitimate, the seller's organization would be expected to bear any incremental costs to correct the situation or to prevent further problems. It is recommended that rather than switch suppliers – work with the supplier to improve their performance. The supplier has a vested interest in doing so. They will also improve their performance for *all* their customers and potential customers. A part of the multiplier or ripple effect in the market similar to the benefits found in quality management.

Pre and Post Contract Supplier Evaluations

Pre-contract Evaluations

A very common business practice is the evaluation of potential suppliers. The traditional assessments are based on the four factors of price, quality, delivery, and service. Additionally, more specifics related to the nature of the goods or service needs are appraised for brand preference, compatibility, standardization, technical advantages, or other product/ service attributes. Evaluations are an important phase of the due diligence phase conducted by private and public sector buying organizations. There can be a substantial amount of time and resources dedicated to this phase by sales groups at the behest of the buying organization.

In the past few years, assessment tools for pre-contract processes can involve comprehensive questionnaires for the screening of potential suppliers for other business relationship values. Often a series of questions are issued by a buying organization which considers the types of CSR and sustainability practices that are being conducted by sellers of goods or services across their respective supply chains. The questions typically will focus on workplace conditions and practices for domestic and or foreign sources, workplace diversity, and environmental commitments and recognized international standards. This gives a sense of the socio/ economic values being brought to the table.

These screening questionnaires, which can appear intimidating, invite responsible suppliers to tell their story which goes beyond the pricing and quality of the goods and services they provide. A properly weighted evaluation on the part of the buyer seeks to identify those suppliers that give back to the community in the various activities they may be involved in.

Site visits are usually conducted by the buying organization to validate claims wherever possible as a part of the short-listing phase. Third party certification of business practices may be required to validate working conditions where outsourcing or offshoring is involved. Product samples or trials and other documentation to validate product/service claims are commonly provided. Subsequently the information gathered in the screening can form a part of the final contract negotiations in the terms and conditions.

The purpose is to identify and reward those suppliers that connect with the economic, environmental, and social values to increase the value proposition. These are the companies that provide the leadership to balance their business model to reflect CSR values in a holistic model. The challenge for the buyer in the weighting is to be objective to quantify the values in the overall value proposition and remain competitive.

Most suppliers must agree to be audited for compliance to supplier codes of conduct throughout the period of the contract prior to an award of business. Senior executives of the sales organization are asked to sign off on this issue which binds the partners to these conditions of performance.

AsiaInspection Ltd., as an example, audits hundreds of foreign factories each year. Their services are used to check on compliance with codes of conduct, work and safety conditions, as well as quality inspections. *AsiaInspection* reports back to their clients are a critical part of a credible CSR strategy.

Post-contract Evaluations

Market leader *Procter & Gamble* introduced a sustainability scorecard for the suppliers it contracts with in 2010. While not entirely new in the field, it is still an important step in business when brand managers take these steps to add legitimacy to the sustainability movement.

With 400+ key suppliers to manage, the introduction of the *P&G* assessment tool is to measure their suppliers' ability to conserve water, reduce waste and emissions. The process will take a year-over-year approach and look for continuous improvement – analogous to quality management practices. *P&G's* strategy was likely influenced by one of its major customers – *Walmart*. As an example of the ripple effect, the *P&G* scorecard is estimated to impact 75,000 businesses across its supply chain.

Walmart, with over 60,000 suppliers began to assess its supplier base following the Carbon Disclosure Project guidelines in 2009. *Walmart* has a series of questions which asks its suppliers to address under the categories of energy and climate, material efficiency, natural resources, and people and community. As a corporation with a tremendous ability to affect pricing and standards, *Walmart* is using their screening tools to identify savings through more responsible practices.

While there is an increase in reporting and compliance costs for *Walmart's* and *P&G's* suppliers in the short-term it should drive out internal and externality costs in the long-term. The pre and post-contract process is the means while more responsible business practices are the end. In all of this, profitability must be inclusive.

 ## Stage #7 - Staying Current

Once a company takes on the CSR responsibility, it must continue to do so for as long as they continue to operate. To do otherwise would make it appear disingenuous and simply self-serving. That's why strategic choices must be made carefully. No one company or solution will solve all of the problems. The sharing of demonstrated results will help drive increased support across many sectors.

While we shouldn't expect organizations to be perfect, we must demand that they act responsibly. Adapting leading practices in business management functions is one way to demonstrate commitment.

Make no mistake it will be work to stay current. An example can be as simple as your disposable coffee cups. Paper coffee cups appear to be recyclable although they have a thin polyethylene layer on the inside surface. There is Polylactic acid (PLA), which may sound bad but it is derived from renewable cornstarch. PLA is a viable alternative to paper, plastic or Styrofoam. Yet, you also have to know that in order for biodegradable food wares such as forks, knives and spoons to be viable they must decompose within a reasonable period of time. Many products will claim to be biodegradable, but few actually are. Another form of greenwashing. As you can see it requires a commitment to stay current so linking up to organizations who make that their job or other CSR advocates in your industry is essential.

When the influential players in any sector take on this type of leadership role to address sustainability, it also triggers the multiplier or ripple effect – they affect more than their supply chain. The producers or distributors or manufacturers typically extend the benefit to all. If you are able to reduce emissions by working with a courier company – not only does your company benefit but all of that courier's customers benefit – along with their employees and the greater community within which they operate.

Wikipedia defines a *Best Practice* as a technique, method, process, activity, incentive or reward that is believed to be more effective at delivering a particular outcome than any other when applied to a particular condition or circumstance. I think it is fair to state that many of today's best practices will not be tomorrow's best practices. It's therefore essential to stay abreast of changes as they occur in each industry and sector.

Where

to focus first?

Where to Focus First?

In business, it is not simply a matter of who should be accomplishing sustainability (we all should), but where can we put our actions to have the greatest impact. The below list is the order in which all of us should be thinking in terms of where to focus first.

1. Emission Inventory
2. Reducing Packaging
3. Local Sourcing
4. Transportation Controls
5. Choice Editing/Retailers
6. Retrofitting Buildings
7. Reduce the Use of Chemicals
8. Green Office Products and Services

 #1 Focus: Emission Inventory

There's no getting away from it: industry generates emissions. While not all industries are the big smoke stack pollutants, emissions are the very poster child of all that is harmful to the planet.

Many claim that producing emissions is simply the cost of doing business and keeping the economy running. It is their right. However, there is increasingly a social pushback to demand that any company that produces emissions must also pay for this "right."

This provides a whole new inventory category for businesses to work with: calculating the theoretical amount of green house gas (GHG) emissions that they produce on an annual basis. GHGs include water vapor, carbon dioxide, methane, nitrous oxide, ozone, and sulphur hexafluoride.

In order to understand how to reduce your emissions and be sustainable, corporations must learn how to measure their emissions. They must reduce wherever possible and offset where they exceed the limits. The base line calculations determine the amount of carbon tax that will eventually be levied.

Carbon neutrality is the term used to describe what is done to remove as much carbon dioxide from the atmosphere as an organization puts into it. The overall goal of carbon neutrality is to achieve a zero carbon footprint.

There are three types of emission inventory:
- ✓ Scope 1—*Direct* emissions, typically from firing boilers, furnaces and vehicular emissions.
- ✓ Scope 2—*Indirect* emissions, such as GHGs from electricity used to provide power to a facility.
- ✓ Scope 3—*Other indirect* emissions. These result from the activities of the institution but are not owned or controlled by them such as energy found in new construction and existing buildings and infrastructure such as concrete, HVAC systems, emissions related to food production. Also, contractor owned vehicles, employee business travel or outsourced activities. It also includes chemical

or technological uses, waste generation and disposal, fertilizers and paper. **Note:** Scope 3 emissions are closely related to the activities under a supply management's portfolio.

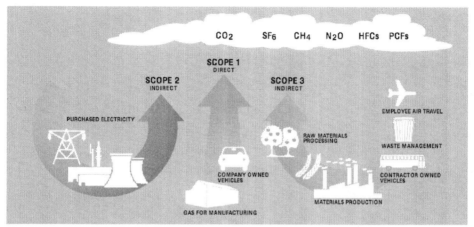

3 Scopes of a Greenhouse Gas Emissions Inventory *Source: New Zealand Business Council for Sustainable Development, The challenges of greenhouse gas emissions: The "why" and "how" of accounting and reporting for GHG emissions (2002, August), figure 3, p. 10.*

Controlling Emissions Impact

It has been and still is up to governments to set the standards and enforce laws that make companies accountable, usually through either through cap and trade programs or carbon tax credits. A cap and trade system is a means by which reductions in greenhouse gas (GHG) emissions can be implemented. It involves creating a market where GHG emission allowances can be bought and sold by entities, better facilitating the reduction of GHGs in a way that prevents inflexible limitations on economic activity.

The cap and trade system is pegged to the maximum level of CO2 emissions that a company can emit. The ceiling is lowered over time to hit optimal levels agreed to by the government. Levels can be set by industry or market sector. Supporters argue that the government should set the cap and trade with input from scientists and climatologists as to what those levels should be. Detractors of the cap and trade programs suggest that it is simply too difficult to calculate, measure, monitor, and adjust such measures.

Cap and trade programs may also consider carbon sequestration. Carbon sequestration means pumping CO_2 into underground storage facilities for long-term storage. It is now being done as the technology is available. It is costly, but is one means of managing tons of CO_2 emissions that otherwise would spew into the atmosphere. Companies who do this can trade for carbon credits on the market.

The basic premise is to measure emissions, reduce wherever possible and offset where emissions exceed limits. The baseline calculations determine the amount of carbon taxes that can be levied. The City of Surrey, British Columbia, for example, has committed to reducing its emissions and energy consumption by 20% by 2020. They have explored opportunities to move towards carbon neutral by investing in local projects that benefit their community and region.

Although both carbon taxes and cap and trade programs generate a lot of debate, the US experience with reducing sulfur dioxide (SO_2) emissions in the early '90s provides a good learning model. The focus at the time was acid rain that polluted soil and water, affecting the health of forests and aquatic life. The prime driver of these emissions was the burning of fossil fuels. Today SO_2 emissions have been substantially reduced. The task now at hand is to deal with the equally harmful CO_2 emissions.

Carbon disclosure has been accepted as a requirement but whether it will be a tax or a trade solution is still unclear. Whatever direction governments take, the focus should be on environmental protection, and not simply as a new revenue stream.

Being Ahead of the Game in Emissions Impact

In 2010, Marius Kloppers, the CEO of BHP Billiton, announced a preemptive strategy of asking for a carbon tax to be imposed on its Australian mining operations in order to be competitive. Kloppers believed it is inevitable that a global carbon tax model is necessary to reduce the level of GHGs. For a CEO to make this type of an announcement was quite surprising.

It also signals to the Australian government that reducing emissions requires government and private sector agreements in principle. The consumers will pay for carbon tax increases through consumption. However, it also requires an internalization of the cost of coal and other mining operations as an outcome. The comments from Kloppers will be closely followed to see whether it was simply a good public relations move, or if it is a signal from a global leader who believes it is better to influence policy before the policy is imposed unilaterally by a government.

In addition, insurance companies are writing policies that put a value on the political risks investors face in a global economy. They are researching risks associated with the potential effects of climate change from a business perspective. This only confirms the growing concern of the effect on our world of emissions and need to address this through carbon offset or through a carbon credit system.

Out of the Penalty Box in Emissions Impact

What could be a better match than hockey players facing off against global warming! In partnership with the Canadian *David Suzuki Foundation*, the National Hockey League Players' Association (NHLPA) created a Carbon Neutral Challenge in 2008. Today more than 500 professional players purchase carbon credits to offset the travel emissions associated with playing professional hockey.

"I'm very proud that we've offset more than 4,200 tons of carbon emissions this season, which is like taking 840 cars off the road for a year," said Andrew Ference, the *Boston Bruins'* defenseman who initiated the NHLPA Carbon Neutral Challenge. "But best of all, I'm hearing of more and more players in the dressing rooms talking about 'going green'."

When high profile NHL players go on the offensive for environmental protection, it sends a clear message to other industries that it's time to get into the game of corporate responsibility. It creates good media as well as being good for the planet.

Reducing Company Emissions

Are you aware of the green house gas (GHG) emissions that your organization produces on an annual basis? This includes water vapor, carbon dioxide, methane, nitrous oxide, ozone, and sulfur hexafluoride in all three scopes as outlined earlier. Having an awareness of your emissions allows you to understand taxes in order to effectively reduce greenhouse gas emissions.

You can start almost anywhere. For example, the push from hardware and software developers is to reduce the energy requirements for servers. Technology, including water-cooled systems replacing air-cooled equipment, is becoming cost effective and provides paybacks through lower energy consumption and therefore lower costs. Energy smart servers are saving up to 50% of the power requirements over conventional models.

Most organizations are going to require external expertise on the intricacy of measuring and calculating emissions. Guidance can be found in the ISO 14064 standards. If a company has an ISO program of an earlier generation, they may want to contact their ISO registrar or provider and engage in an emission calculation study.

Additionally, supply professionals should be able to facilitate discussions on the overall assessment of cost and operational changes required to meet ISO green house gas standards.

Third party service providers such as *Offsetters* can help by offering sustainability and carbon-management solutions to offset a company's environmental impact.

Questions to Answer to Reduce Your Emissions Inventory

1. Have you figured out your GHG sources (Sources 1-3) to analyze your reduction strategy?
2. Can you be ahead of the game (regulations or taxes to come) and agree to lead the industry?
3. Have you looked at realistic offsetting and ways to implement it creatively?
4. Can you create a competitive challenge to help get the word out?

5. Have you contacted an organization that can give you expert help whether it is implementing ISO or using third party service providers such as *Offsetters?*

 ## #2 Focus: Reducing Packaging

In North America the accumulative mountains of waste are a shared responsibility by business and consumers. We generate more than we can possible recycle or hide in landfills. Everyone knows about it but in general few are doing a lot about the problem. One of the symbols of waste is the over usage of plastic bags and related plastic products. In May 2007, the province of Ontario, Canada, began a program to eliminate plastic bags which are being used at the rate of 7 million bags per day. Major retailers such as *Dominion* and *A&P* are providing incentives to get their customers to convert to reusable bags.

- In Ireland they charge people $.22 per bag. 2003
- In San Francisco banned plastic bags in grocery stores and pharmacies. 2007
- Leaf Rapids, Manitoba, became the first entire city to ban plastic bags. 2007
- *IKEA UK* stopped issuing plastic bags and charges customers $.05 per plastic bag while trying to get them to buy a reusable bag. 2006
- *IKEA US* adopted the same program in 2007 which led to a 95% reduction in plastic bags
- Taiwan has banned restaurants from using plastic knives, forks, and spoons. 2007

- Italy has banned the use of plastic bags being provided by retailers to their customers. Plastic bags could only be used until inventories were depleted,. 2011

Many stores still issue plastic bags at no charge for shoppers. Other stores will issue a bag and charge for their customers for them. Either way plastic bags are still in circulation. The use of reusable carrying bags by shoppers is popular and growing. The elimination of plastic bags is a slow behavioral change issue for retailers. Though the responsibility is largely in the hands of the individual consumer there are the choices or elimination of choices that retailers can and should be sponsoring.

If you are a retailer or work with retailers, introduce the above examples and ideas for how you can curb the use of plastic bag usage. The elimination of plastic bags is evolving into the replacement of many different kinds of oil-based packaging materials including styrofoam. This trend will likely continue as alternatives are less costly and provide sustainable solutions. However, be wary that they are in the long term sustainable. Even if they are biodegradable, some choices may not be sustainable in their processes or harm-free in the long run, so do your research.

Work with your suppliers to reduce packaging as much as possible at the source. Packaging takes three main forms:
1. Primary: the consumer wrapping or container
2. Secondary: packaging that may be used to contain the primary packaging used in distribution
3. Transit: the packaging or handling containers such as wooden pallets, shrink-wrap or cargo containers for bulk shipments

As much packaging as possible should be eliminated at source. All packaging should be left at or returned to the point-of-purchase location for disposal. If the cost of returned packaging is borne by the producer or manufacturer then these costs will be internalized and better methods of protecting goods or more eco-friendly materials will be found.

One of the principles of the European Packaging guidelines is that, "used packaging is a valuable resource and should not be mismanaged." These guidelines were developed in 1999. North American business can learn a lot from other jurisdictions. The Euro model may not be perfect but it is another tool towards introducing sustainable business practices.

In 2014, the Province of British Columbia introduced its Multi-Material BC (MMBC) print and packaging collection system. In essence the cost of disposal of the materials will be borne by the producers based on a cost per kg for the larger producers. Inequities abound in the proposed system but it is a step in the right direction with costs being internalized across the supply chain. The initial program will also include aerosol containers, drink cups and milk cartons. MMBC is an industry driven not-for-profit organization with a private sector governance.

Embedding sustainability into existing contracts is totally doable. Supply professionals DO NOT need to wait until the contract expires or when they go to market with an RFP to embed sustainability criteria into their contracts. That was the case for me when working for The University of British Columbia (2008). The University and *Acklands-Grainger (A-G)* have a preferred vendor agreement. Our Sustainability Advisor, having worked with *A-G* previously was fairly certain they would help facilitate ideas to reduce packaging and address the carbon footprint.

We organized a brain storming session with the *A-G* National Account Manager, a Branch Manager and the Key Account sales representative. We quickly identified reusable totes as the answer to reduce packaging and eliminating daily deliveries to address the carbon footprint.

A-G orders their inventory stock in large quantities from manufacturers similar to bulk buying and stores them in strategically located warehouses. The University's orders are picked, placed in totes and shipped to UBC twice per week. By eliminating the packaging and placing the goods into reusable totes we managed to save both *A-G* and UBC the cost of packaging materials extra labor and the cost of disposing of the waste packaging. The consolidation of two shipments per week also reduced fuel consumption by 90%.

Sometimes reusable totes are not possible and companies are looking for environmental alternatives. Specific alternatives are available for different applications. Bioplastics such as Polylactic acid (PLA) derived from renewable cornstarch are a viable alternative to paper and PVC plastics or polystyrene foam – although there can be limitations with hot products. PLA is widely used for clam-shell type food containers and can be formed into bottle shapes.

Starch-based packaging made from tapioca or potato starch is used for disposable plates and cutlery. Sugar cane and cornhusks can be used for non-rigid packaging and containers. There are many more responsible material options where packaging is required. Again, these new products require research on their biodegradability. Are they approved by the universities and scientists that study impacts and the environmental groups that publicize the research? This is up to SCM and your CSR team to know the best alternatives to present.

Hats off to *Coca-Cola* for its new *PlantBottle* made from sugar cane and molasses. The beverage industry needs to develop more responsible packaging and containers for its products that are not derivatives of fossil fuels. Renewable sources of materials are a key to managing costs and mitigating environmental degradation.

 ### *Questions to Answer to Reduce Packaging*

1. How are you going to help control or limit the use of unnecessary plastics from your supply chain?
2. What other ways can PVC based-packaging be reduced or replaced with biodegradable packaging?
3. What resources will you use to ensure alternative packaging truly is sustainable and biodegradable?

 ## #3 Focus: Local Sourcing

Local sourcing has long been the bane of buyers for good reasons. Paying higher prices in order to support businesses based on their postal code proximity alone was never a good strategy. The practice fell out of grace as the value seldom justified the price differences. The most recent economic crisis has always been used as an excuse for buying "local" in order to protect self-serving interests of those within a target jurisdiction. This is short-term thinking at its worst: Buy-Canadian or Buy-American or Buy-British. This knee-jerk spend mentality can lead to the increase of tariffs on imports to protect inefficient domestic producers.

Long-term economic weakness is the result of protectionism. For instance Canadian shoe manufacturers can only supply less than 1% of the retail market yet all Canadian shoe customers pay 3-5% duty on all other shoes that must be imported. This protects a handful of Eastern Canadian shoe manufacturers. In another example a Toronto-based company *IPEX Inc.* was exporting pipe to the United States market for decades and landed a contract to supply plastic piping for a new health-care center at the Camp Pendleton Marine base in California. But the piping was ripped out of the ground because the pipes are branded with the words *Made in Canada*. There are other examples where the reverse was done on the other side of the border to *Made in USA* products. These decisions literally waste resources already consumed to make the first order and the political pressure outweighs the business sense or environmental considerations.

While it may be more supportive to a local economy to buy products from within a political jurisdiction it may make more economic and sustainable interest to buy where the travel time is the most direct. There isn't a clear answer on this subject. Should a Vancouver-based health care facility bring in medical supplies from Edmonton or Toronto which are 24–72 hours away or bring them up from Seattle which is only 3 hours away? Tariffs or trade agreements tend to be protective of political and economic interests while they may actually be contributing to greater emission problems by where we source. However, there are other areas where industries and companies should always be looking for local sources and your CSR teams needs to plug into what is right for them.

Mining and Forestry

In operations for resource-based commodities, such as mining and forestry, it does make sense to have local sources in order to minimize inventory and ensure service levels. Extraction industries in rural or remote locations require a large percentage of local business for greater assurance of supply and in case of emergencies to avoid unplanned shut downs. This allows the larger community- or regional-based employer to reduce their inventory investment, provide employment which enhanced the community, and afforded social programs such as schools and hospitals and civic services and amenities.

Sherritt International Corporation which is mining in Madagascar committed to building lemur bridges to protect these animals near their mining operations – before beginning the project. They installed state-of-the-art biomedical monitoring to assess the health of the lemur population and contribute to a viable habitat.

KGHM International's social responsibility policy states that they define success in their mining operations where employees, contractors, local and indigenous people, and other stakeholders commit to working together to develop resources.

As a result of its poor environmental record in the late '90s, *BHP Billiton* acknowledged its shortcomings in the mining industry and established a Forum on Corporate Responsibility. The forums invite input from various stakeholders such as technical experts from multiple geographical locations to assess the potential impact of *BHP* on society. This commitment is embedded permanently in their stakeholder engagement program. The forum tackles thorny issues on climate change, energy, anti-corruption, and transparency to name a few.

Food Purveyors and Restaurants

There is growing interest in local and organic produce and the *100-Mile Diet* is a popular trend in many cities. Buying locally makes sense on a seasonal basis for all of the basics that go along with healthy nutrition through accessibility to fresh products. Most food was organic until scientists concocted synthetic chemicals and fertilizers to increase production around 1940. They encouraged the use of DDT to control pests and boost production—a fateful choice for the birds and the bees. Organic foods are very popular, and while there are legislated standards for organic food production, there is no comprehensive legislation to manage the organic food market to date. The market must rely on voluntary compliance by virtuous farmers and producers.

A growing trend towards an increase in local sourcing is going to occur where we factor in emissions related to transportation costs. This expands the value to go beyond the more intuitive cost factors and considers the CO_2 effect on decisions. Food purveyors are naturally the ones to see how this makes the most sense and they see consumers favoring local food supplies for a sustainable community. Seasonal fruits and vegetables are no longer seasonal when we have access to them year round. The importing of fruits and vegetables to date typically excludes the emission costs associated with the transportation. This will change the economics of the business once these costs become a part of the cost of the produce. In turn, it may create a demand for local seasonal produce when it is fresh and available and a return to preserving produce.

The *Hasai Restaurant* in Singhampton, Ontario, Canada, has combined farming with its restaurant and bakery. *Hasai's* menu is based strictly on locally grown ingredients including grains, vegetables, and meats. To complement these items *Hasai* buys organic products from local farmers and gardeners. Chef Stadtlander's philosophy supports a holistic model from the *Eigensinn Farm* to the creative dishes he serves.

The *Farm* does *not* hire employees. It offers apprentices the opportunity to learn to tend animals, work in the garden, and operate a smoke house. With no salary, only room and board being provided, it is a way for rising chefs to gain a better understanding of the importance of food that goes beyond just cooking.

This business model is an example of the successful niche, which benefits from servicing customers who are seeking a food experience based on a sustainable food chain. The restaurant also presents an informative news program linking agriculture and foods as a part of their philosophical commitment to promote health and dining. *Hasai* was voted one of Canada's best new restaurants in 2010.

If you think that getting volunteers to work on your organic farm is only for niche restaurateurs you would be incorrect. The 30-year old *World-Wide Opportunities on Organic Farms* (WWOOF) organization promotes travel and education on organic farming techniques. If you are willing to put in 4-5 hours per day for 4-5 days per week for food and accommodations, there are over 800 WWOOF host farm locations in Canada to choose from. WWOOF network of programs is in 50 countries and integrates health, foods, lifestyles, and cultural diversity.

The University of British Columbia (UBC) Food Services group looked at packaging, transportation, and inputs such as water, energy, and soybeans and wastewater discharge as a full Life Cycle Assessment (LCA-$) approach. As a part of the summary of the findings:

FOOD PRODUCT	PRICE PER kg	CO2 EMISSIONS PER kg
Tofu	$4.45	2.7 kg
Beef	$7.00	22.0 kg
Organic Beef	$9.40	*
Pork Chops	$7.00	12.0 kg
Organic Pork Chops	$35.00	*
Chicken	$7.55	7.0 kg
Organic Chicken	$8.00	*

*The industrialized preparing of the animal's food and the transport (local sourcing) are the major differences in CO2 for organic versus conventional yet the other sustainability positives for organic are enormous: http://timeforchange.org/ http://www.ewg.org/meateatersguide/

You can see that not all the costing comes out the way you might expect. Putting more tofu items on the menu was an obvious, thrifty choice. The savings for using a tofu alternative may allow for a splurge on higher priced local organics for another part of the budget. And, to understand that organic is not always a lot more expensive, as in the chicken, can also determine better choices.

The UBC study reiterates that the business case is there to measure the opportunities which are available in the market. The food group saw a trend, located a competitive and responsible source for a protein alternative, took the Life Cycle Assessment (LCA) approach to determine the overall effect, and was able to meet a trend which contributes to a healthier life style and ensures fiscal needs are being met.

Food is one area where local sourcing makes a great deal of sense, however, local sourcing, emissions analysis and transportation controls can apply to any business, for nearly any supply. Doing a full LCA may require some expert advice and analysis but figuring out whether you can buy local without losing competitive cost advantages is part of the new model that all organizations and SCM need to factor in. There may already be a study out there, like the UBC study, for your supply challenges that can at least start you thinking outside the box.

Local Materials Energy and Transportation

The traditional industrial and commercial distribution center logistical networks and manufacturing locations were established when oil prices were $20.00-40.00 per barrel – not $140.00+ per barrel. It is not easy to physically relocate a distribution center. It is a relatively easier choice as to which distribution center to buy from.

A building supply company needs a load of lumber in Vancouver. The lumber could be delivered from the Canadian town of Prince George or from the closer American town of Bellingham. If oil prices are ~$200 per barrel and emissions must be accounted for trade offs will need to be made. But, the use of indigenous local materials could be a more responsible decision than importing alternative materials such as biomass gasification systems.

Biomass gasification systems using organic solid materials or bio solids as the fuel source can help to solve local municipal waste problems while providing cost effective and sustainable solutions to energy costs. They use local waste products or materials for their fuel source thereby providing flexibility for geographical locations. It mitigates transportation of fuel and enables cogeneration of energy options. The use of wood waste as a biomass source in Ontario and British Columbia where forestry and lumber are strategic economic drivers is a good example of drawing on local materials as opposed to using other fossil fuels. Your CSR Team

needs to be aware of this alternative so they can look into it as an option for both your company or your suppliers.

Since 2006, *Tolko Industries* plywood operation in Kamloops B.C. has saved 12k tons of green house gas emissions and $1.5M on fuel costs per year through their investment in wood gasification technology. In 2007, The University of British Columbia's Kelowna campus relied on geothermal energy to replace its natural gas plant reducing 1900 tons of carbon dioxide emissions per year. These are examples of how organizations are designing their infrastructure needs on local energy sources rather than transporting fossil-based fuels to their locations.

Productivity and Local Economies

Japanese automakers did not have the luxury of vacant land mass to expand their production facilities. This in turn contributed to their development of the just-in-time manufacturing model that made their vehicles more competitive and substantially reduced inventory investments. Greater productivity and efficiency almost always creates greater sustainability and this can often be tied into local economics and local sourcing.

The emergence of Italian mini-mills in the steel industry, for example, was driven by high cost associated with the logistics of getting product to shipping ports. The mini-mills were designed to consume less energy, be less capital-intensive and rely on scrap metals as a main source of materials. It was essentially a more sustainable and competitive industry.

For ethical procurement you must be able to look at all the production efficiency factors and also the externality costs so you can have a true comparison of apples-to-apples costs. Without this analysis economic rewards could go to lower cost foreign producers that are able to offload their externality costs such as work place safety practices or effluent discharge. Domestic sources are not able to do that due to local regulations. External CSR expertise is usually required to address these issues with a comprehensive strategy.

 Questions to Answer to Increase Your Local Sourcing

1. Are you in an industry where local sourcing makes sense both economically and for sustainability?
2. With each procurement, do you have a way to analyze which has more CSR value, a local sourcing or another sourcing? Are your policies written to allow for this?
3. Are there ways for you to leverage local alternative energy sources and local transportation opportunities?
4. Can you lead the industry by creating a local efficiency model?

 ## #4 Focus: Transportation Controls

According to Nancy Knight, Assistant Manager Corporate Strategy for the Greater Vancouver Regional District (GVRD), transportation accounts for 40-50% of GHGs. The GVRD consists of 21 municipalities and 2.5 million people. Reducing GHGs by 25% is one of the GVRD goals. This is a significant undertaking to benefit business and consumers alike. But what should you be looking at for your transportation controls to make the greatest impacts.

1. Corporate Travel
2. Offsetting
3. Telecommuting
4. Courier and Cartage

Business Travel

According to the *International Air Transport Association* (IATA) air travel contributes 2% of the global CO2 emissions today and is expected to climb to 3% by 2050. Not what we would like to hear. IATA represents its member's interests before US and Canadian government executive and legislative bodies.

IATA has outlined a strategy to address climate change issues based on technology operations infrastructure and economic measures. This implies a coordinated lobbying effort to ensure that the air travel industry is doing what it can to address issues within their mandate. As business people we need to have a complementary strategy to affect change also. Responsible travel programs are necessary and are often connected with supply management through a service contract management role.

Responsible travel programs look at strategies and tactical activities that can mitigate the environmental and economic costs incurred when travelling on business. Corporate travel service agreements should include information sharing that informs travelers of the options they should consider reducing their carbon footprint related to travel and accommodations. Electronic updates are efficient and effective to perform this function.

Responsible travel management programs include stays at *green* hotels, e-tickets, e-invoices, e-mail updates, rental of hybrid vehicles, car/taxi sharing, and the use of public transit and rail in high traffic corridors. Routes such as the Toronto/Montreal or Vancouver/Seattle are ideal for rail commutes. Work with your corporate travel service provider to expand the services and promote responsible travel programs within your organization. More assertive actions include carbon-offset agreements for the requisite travel trips.

Carbon Offsetting

Third party offset organizations can easily provide calculating and providing types of service that will offset the CO_2 damage. The easiest and least intrusive means of accommodating an offset fee is at source such as including the value in the ticket price. *Harbour Air* was one of the first to adopt this strategy in October 2007. Because it was easy customers welcomed and supported this commitment.

The carbon offset fees collected by *Harbour Air* from its customers were remitted to a third party not-for-profit carbon offset service provider *Offsetters Climate Neutral Society* (*Offsetters*). *Offsetters* found a project where these funds could be used to reduce CO_2 emissions. *Offsetters* contacted the *Delta View Habilitation Centre,* an extended care facility in B.C. and the funds were invested in a ground source heat pump for the HVAC system installation. This energy efficient system reduced emissions by 75%. The additional cost of the ground source heat pump when compared to a traditional gas and electric system was *offset* by the original *Harbour Air* carbon offset fees.

In addition, and an important part of the carbon offset cycle, the ground source heat pump project was validated by *A.D. Williams Engineering Inc.* as generating actual and long-term GHG emissions.

Other offset programs can be negotiated as a portion of the annualized cost. An example is where your airline partner can provide an annual rebate based on the cost of ticket purchases which you in turn remit to a third party carbon aggregator.

Carbon calculators provide insight into the cost of travel for an individual and provide an estimate for the cost to offset the emissions. Using the model provided by *Carbon Friendly Solutions™* a person flying from Vancouver to Toronto and return would pay ~ $21.00 to offset the emissions where travel cannot be avoided. The cost of a coach class return ticket to Toronto is ~ $850.00. The offsetting cost is 2% of the ticket price. Having customers *voluntarily* take the steps to offset their emission contributions is a nice idea. A more effective solution would be to include the offset fees in the ticket prices. This would capture more of the benefits and most travelers would not notice a 2% fee.

Teleconferencing and Telecommuting

Other strategies to better manage air travel should include increased use of technologies such as video conferencing. A professional association wants to hold a national conference. The cost of air travel is escalating and virtual conferencing technology is becoming lower in costs. It is simple to set up these systems and requires low IT support. Airlines, hotels, educational institutions and conference centers may have to reposition their services in order to have an economic model that is sustainable. Remote access 65" HDTV monitors and surround-sound systems enable information sharing in a more robust and interactive format offering a "just like being there" encounter.

This system is used on a regular basis between university researchers globally eliminating the need for travel without compromising the quality of the communications. The investment for the University of British Columbia was $25000 for their system that uses the Internet for connectivity at no additional charge, and they make their HDTV system available to external organizations on an hourly charge basis, recouping their costs.

Telecommuting is also being adopted in many businesses with technology as an enabler. We are faced with employees driving farther to work due to the proximity of affordable housing. In many cases commuting times were in excess of an hour. Inclement weather often led to longer commutes and cancelled meetings. According to *Avaya Inc.*, an employee solution provider organization, there are 800,000 Canadians who telecommute full time, with over 2.0 million Canadian workers telecommuting at least one day per week. In the US, the figures are well over double those in Canada.

In addition, telecommuting is providing a whole new area for companies to compete by reducing operating costs. *JetBlue,* the US airline started in 2001, was one of the early adopters of this as a human resource strategy. *JetBlue* customer support is handled online and by way of many employees working out of their homes in Utah. Reduced office space and overhead is also a significant cost saving.

I initiated telecommuting for staff in two public sector organizations. The municipal entity was very much against this type of work arrangement at the time. Implementing the idea in absence of an HR policy can lead to chaos. The union was against telework as it could conflict with working conditions hours of work and was inequitable as not all employees would be able to participate due to job duty requirements.

In one organization I introduced the informal municipal telecommuting initially only based on special needs of two staff members. One person

146

we set up was a work-at-home father and the other individual had health issues that restricted her ability due to medical treatments. Both employees contributed value to the operations and the department was able to meet its services. The work they did was the drafting of proposals and contracts. To date this municipal organization has not adopted a telecommuting policy.

The other organization was much more supportive. We worked with HR to develop a policy and start a telecommuting pilot program. Starting with this control group within the supply management staff itself we identified who would be telecommuting. There was a formal document signed off by the participating staff that included clear definition of their roles and tasks. Time management and service performance on the part of the home-office staff was critical to the success of the program and successful monitoring. The success we had contributed to a better understanding of the telecommuting pros and cons. We learned from early errors and revised the program as it continued to roll out.

The Cons of Telecommuting

- A perceived fear of productivity loss—it's not for those who need more supervision
- Equity between employees who can telecommute and those who can't

The Pros of Telecommuting

- Hundreds of gallons of gas saved annually, reducing CO_2 emissions.
- Hundreds of dollars saved per employee every year.
- Easier to attract and retain staff with the work-life balance of telecommuting.
- More alert employees who get more rest.
- Less sick days or spreading illness and colds at the workplace.

Courier and Cartage Services

Another great area to look for transportation controls is in looking at your own courier and cartage services. Are they trying to make a difference? As discovered in a study of municipal courier services there are several actions that can be taken by courier operators to reduce their costs and emissions. It's important to see that this is a mutual benefit program between the service provider and the customer. The former saves fuel and improves service capabilities while the latter receives improved services at no extra cost. The learning outcomes revealed the need for a common denominator to compare competing proposals.

The common denominators to determine best value were:

- An estimate of annual km in the service areas
- An estimate of the service provider's average fuel consumption based on the composition of the fleet vehicles
- The cost was based on the required levels of service

To calculate the volume of GHG emissions in tons, the formula is the total number of liters of fuel consumed multiplied by .00236. Traditionally buyers award contracts based on the lowest price. With sustainability they need to define the best value within the 3Es concept.

Service level agreements are useful to identify each party's commitments towards achieving the benefits. This study revealed the multiplier effect whereby all customers benefit when the service provider vigorously applies fuel and safety practices. Idle-free driving programs, good vehicle maintenance and proper tire inflation are keys to success.

Alternative fuels can help with reducing emissions within an urban setting but are not essential to make progress. As hybrid vehicles and optional fuel vehicles become more affordable and as fleet vehicles are replaced there is an inherent economic benefit built in to the cost structure. While it is true there is an additional capital investment it is offset through substantial fuel reduction. Often times it is the operator of the vehicle and not the courier or cartage company that invests in the actual vehicles.

Electric service and delivery vehicles will be game changers in the courier/cartage market. Technical advances are making electric vehicles more affordable and reliable. There will be pressure mounted on utility services and municipalities to provide an energy grid that supports electric vehicles. That will also likely include a pay-as-you-plug-in for the use of energy for recharging electric vehicles. Research is now underway for the self-charging of vehicles.

The use of nitrogen-filled tires is becoming more common. They have been used in mining vehicles, airplane, racecar and commercial truck tires for years. Nitrogen is less prone to leakage which is the main cause of under-inflation. Under-inflation reduces fuel efficiency. Nitrogen keeps the tire temperature lower and does not react with metal rims and the tire rubber, which extends their operating life. The cost is $5.00 to inflate a tire but fuel efficiency has been reported to be ~5%. This can be a significant benefit to fleet managers and it's good for the environment.

Route optimization software is available to provide the most efficient route for delivery vehicles that optimizes the time and fuel consumption ratios. Route logistics used to be left to the expertise of the driver. Leading companies now rely on software to load data on their multi-stop routes and schedules, fleet size, back hauls, distance, fuel consumption rates, cost of fuel, less-than-truck loads, driver scheduling, along with updates on major roads airport and combining with rail and ship modes of transport. The complexity requires investment in order to attain efficiencies and mitigate environmental impact.

An innovative strategy practiced by *UPS* drivers is the idea of no left turns. According to the report *UPS* has trimmed 30 million route miles, 3 million gallons of gas and 32000 metric tons of carbon dioxide emissions. Left turns have been found to waste time and energy so *UPS* has taken as many left turns out of their routes as is possible.

The CEO of *Novex Couriers* in Vancouver, Robert Safrata, positioned his company to benefit from the interest in lower emission vehicles. Safrata's goal is to eventually convert their entire fleet of vehicles to ultra low emission vehicles (ULEV). *Novex* has applied sustainability practices throughout its operations and administrative functions to reduce costs.

As an example, *Novex* took its first hybrid vehicle through the local government testing agency, Air Care. The results showed that for a conventional gasoline-powered courier car, hydrocarbon emissions were reduced by 99.99%, carbon monoxide reduced by 82%, and nitrous oxide by 99.99%! Without having a CSR policy most customers of courier services evaluate heavily on price and quality of service when awarding courier contracts. The cost of emissions becomes an externality cost.

In 2010, *Novex* took delivery of two electric vans for its fleet. Built by the British firm, Smith Electric Vehicles, *Novex* expects to reduce emissions by 58 tons per year and save $25,000 dollars per year in fuel costs by using these newer ultra low emission vehicles.

Questions to Answer to Manage Your Transportation Controls

1. Do you have a sustainable employee travel policy and programs?
2. Have you investigated offsetting?
3. Have you analyzed and created a teleconferencing and a telecommuting policy and program in your organization?
4. Have you looked into your supplier for courier and cartage services to see if they are operating at a higher sustainability level?

#5 Focus: Choice-Editing/Retailers

Rather than requiring customers to choose between traditional or green alternatives some retailers are only selling green or greener items. This is what is called *choice-editing* to provide more sustainable products and materials. Along with the greener choices is the idea of carbon labels.

In the UK, this includes non-sustainable wood being replaced by *Forest Stewardship Council* certified lumber, a 70% increase in the amount of water-based paints, only selling energy-efficient condensing boilers for buildings/homes, and 90% of canned tuna is *dolphin-safe*. Interestingly, organic food products still face a high barrier due to the perceived price versus the benefits of organics and are being marketed as niche items. Again in the UK, big box home improvement retailer, *B&Q*, has stopped selling standard propane-fuelled patio heaters.

UK retailer, Tesco, in early 2008 began putting carbon-count labels on varieties of branded juice, potatoes, energy-efficient light bulbs and washing detergent, stating the quantity of CO_2 equivalent put into the atmosphere by their manufacture and distribution. The province of British Columbia banned 75 and 100-watt incandescent light bulbs in 2011. Consumers were forced to buy more energy efficient compact fluorescent bulbs. This is not without controversy but is a growing trend with consumers.

The food industry will be faced with a considerable task if CO_2 emissions related to refrigeration are required as a part of the labeling. Regardless, food costs could increase by requiring companies to internalize the refrigeration costs, attached directly to food production and distribution.

There is a trend towards providing the amount of calories in fast food products to influence behavior. New York City's Mayor Bloomberg was a strong advocate for informing consumers and increasing the awareness of healthier diets. In Canada and the US choices are left up to the consumer where decisions are strongly influenced by price.

In 2014, *Kraft Foods* announced it was replacing sorbic acid with natamycin as a natural mold inhibitor in its *full-fat* American cheese slices. *Subway* says it is removing the chemical azodicarbonamide from its bread. The chemical is also used *in Starbucks, Pizza Hut*, and *McDonald's* products and is an ingredient in yoga mats. These ingredients are allowed by the FDA. *Kraft* says it is in response to increased consumer desire for more natural foods.

Choice-editing is a combination of marketing and consumerism. Informed consumers may make better choices if they know about the benefits but it has a slow adoption rate. The elimination of harmful or wasteful products has a more immediate effect and the technical solutions require little behavioral change on the part of the consumer. When there was finally a decision to remove lead from gasoline and paint products several years ago for obvious health reasons, no one noticed but everyone has benefitted. If you are in a retail organization then it is time to introduce this idea to your product lines, also bring it up to any relevant associations and even introduce it to your competitors. Often entire industries around a product can agree to choice edit.

 ## Questions to Answer to Implement Choice-Editing

1. Can your own product sales and services choice-edit for your buyers?
2. Do the retailers you support also support conscious choice-editing for a better planet?

 # #6 Focus: Retrofitting Buildings

We are wasting our energy. Energy management looks at the supply side (power source such as hydroelectric gas wind or other alternatives) and the demand side. The latter looks at the production of power, its efficiency conservation and recovery methodologies. Retrofitting buildings is a part of carbon emission management operational strategies. The potential energy savings are reported to be in the range of $10 - 20\%$ through infrastructure upgrades combined with maintenance and operating practice reviews. The goal is to reduce the amount of GHGs.

When a building needs to be demolished, the more common practice would be to demolish it and the material would end up in a landfill site. A more responsible option is *deconstruction* by salvaging existing resources: concrete and bricks can be turned into rubble material for backfill on local projects, lumber can be reused for other construction purposes, steel can be recycled, all which increase landfill capacity. Deconstruction costs more in time and labor but may be better than wasting previously harvested resources and promotes local employment.

The design of a building arguably controls 60-70% of the buildings operating costs. This is the driver behind the retrofitting of current facilities. Programs to retrofit can be managed with in-house resources, contracted energy service companies, or outsourced comprehensive programs.

Mountain Equipment Co-op's new retro-fitted Ottawa store may well be the most environmentally friendly retail building in Canada. By recycling and using highly efficient building materials – such as straw bales – the Ottawa location will consume one half the energy that a conventional store of comparable size would. Although the cost was ~10% more than that of traditional construction *Mountain Equipment Co-op* expects to recover the investment in 10 to 12 years through energy savings.

Mountain Equipment Co-op's Ottawa outlet was the first retail store in Canada that complies with Canada's C-2000 Green Building Standard. That means the new store was designed and built to have the least possible impact on the environment. For example, of the original 40-year old building that was renovated to house the new stores, fully 75% (by weight) of the original materials were retained. Timber was reclaimed from the St. Lawrence River and used for new construction in the building. About 80% of all the materials used in the construction were obtained within a 500-mile radius of the site to minimize the upstream environmental impacts from transportation.

Overall more than 55% of the materials (by weight) in the new building were recycled, cleaned up and reused – including steel beams, cellulose insulation, rock, wool from recycled material, wood from other dismantled buildings, and bricks from the old building on the site.

Equally impressive is the retrofitting of the iconic Empire State Building's 6500 windows. The windows are but one of eight projects which will result in energy savings of 38% or $4.4 million dollars per year. The innovative window design is the brainchild of Kevin Surace, CEO of *Serious Materials*. The process includes the reuse of the original glass and adds a special film and krypton gas to insulate the new windowpanes. Generally, concrete and steel buildings cannot be deconstructed and put back together. They must be reengineered in terms of their energy source HVAC systems, windows, insulation, plumbing, electrical, IT and other supporting services.

This trend to retrofitting will likely continue as it affords cost effective options for building owners and operators over the long term. Building owners and project managers will be working with third party engineering firms on more innovative means of reducing the costs of operating buildings. The objective is to conserve CO_2 emissions while saving costs *enabling* the success of these investment ventures. If retrofits are not undertaken and carbon tax policies are implemented the building operator may end up paying higher costs by having to offset the emissions.

Questions to Answer to Use Retro-fitting

1. Have you done an analysis of the possible benefits of retro-fitting your building?
2. Have you looked at consultants or organizations that can help you in a retro-fit analysis or project?

#7 Focus: Reducing Chemicals

Drawing from research in Europe harmful chemicals are present in almost every product we buy. Awareness of their toxicity and link to human health is important for supply professionals to make informed and better decisions where possible.

Some Chemicals to Be Aware Of

- **CFC:** In the 1970s we became aware of chlorofluorocarbons (CFCs) used as propellants in aerosol paint and coolants that led to a depletion of the ozone layer.
- **HCFC:** Hydro-chlorinated fluorocarbons (HCFCs) replaced CFCs but HCFCs continue to harm the environment and the manufacturers have agreed to phasing out the use of HCFCs – by 2030! HCFCs and variations of this chemical formula are used in HVAC systems

automobile AC systems and many other industrial and commercial applications.

- **Hydrofluoric Acid:** A highly corrosive and contact poison capable of causing death. Inhaling fumes can lead to loss of nerve functions and cardiac arrest.

- **DDT:** DDT is still used in less developed countries. When the last DDT manufacturing facility was decommissioned in the US in 1983 it was shipped to Indonesia where it is currently making DDT. Do your suppliers use Indonesian suppliers?

- **Phthalates:** Banned in Europe but not in Canada or the US Phthalates are the primary ingredients in vinyl and are linked to damage in the human reproductive system, kidney problems, asthma and cancer. Phthalates are present in lubricants, solvents, cosmetics, perfumes, nail polish, paint, packaging materials, children's toys, adult toys and hospital intravenous tubing.

- **Bisphenol A:** Bisphenol A (BPA) is linked to endocrine function health issues and is banned in Canada but not in the USA. BPA is used in polycarbonate plastic drink containers food can liners tableware and in thousands of consumer products as well as dental sealant for children. In 2010, Canada placed BPA on its list of dangerous substances due to its toxicity. Europe, however, did not do likewise citing they could not find "convincing evidence" of neurobehavioral toxicity. The Canadian federal government expects companies to develop contingency plans to prevent BPA from entering the industrial waste stream within 60 days of this announcement. At this time, it still only asked for the plans – not necessarily the actions to be taken.

- **Ethylene glycol monobutyl ether:** Ethylene glycol monobutyl ether is linked to haemolytic anemia. It is use to make paints, cleaning products, textiles, finger nail polish and removers and cosmetics.

- **Acid Orange 24:** Acid Orange 24 an ingredient in cosmetics is linked to cancer and is banned in Europe while Canada is reviewing it along with 22 other similar chemicals.

- **VOCs:** Effective in 2010 mandatory limits will be set for volatile organic compounds (VOCs) used in automotive refinishing products. Collision shops will not be allowed to buy or import non-compliant products after this date. The purpose of the delayed legislation is to allow the use of existing inventories purchased before the effective date of the regulations. VOCs although they have proven to be harmful will not be banned: only reduced in the amount of air pollutants they emit.

- **Chemical Pesticides:** In 2008 a controversial debate was being generated by the Canadian Cancer Society with respect to chemical pesticides used in farm production. The Canadian Cancer Society contends that there is a link to an increase in the presence of cancer in farm workers and the use of pesticides. The CCS bases their findings on epidemiology studies which imply diseases such as colorectal, prostate, lung, ovarian and blood cancers could be expected in farm workers.

- **Cosmetic Pesticides:** Various jurisdictions have banned cosmetic pesticides--pesticides for the purpose of improving or maintaining an aesthetic quality in fruits and vegetables--these same pesticides are applied in far greater quantities in agricultural operations than other pesticides. The provinces of Ontario, Quebec, New Brunswick and Prince Edward Island currently ban the use of non-essential pesticides. Various Canadian municipalities have enacted by-laws that prohibit the use of cosmetic pest controls.

The list of chemicals that could be considered toxic or harmful could consume reams of paper. It serves no further value to belabor the point that buyers may not know which chemicals are included in the products they are importing or using on a daily basis. We rely on Material Safety Data Sheets for compliance with regulations. In Europe they have REACH – Registration Evaluation and Authorization of Chemicals. The focus of REACH is to provide research on existing chemicals as the information is not readily available, and to provide a regulatory system to manage the production import and use of chemicals within Europe. It is likely there will be REACH models adopted in Canada and the US within the next few years. Most of the chemicals are currently legal to import and use. It takes more due diligence to find alternatives.

Akzo Nobel a Dutch company, links the pay of its executives to the position of *Akzo Nobel* on the Dow Jones Sustainability Index (DJSI) for chemical companies. The DJSI are a family of indices evaluating the sustainability performance of the largest 2,500 companies listed on the Dow Jones Global Total Stock Market Index.). The Dutch asset management firm *Robeco* supports *Akzo Nobel's* executive pay strategy as it sees above average results in companies that link remuneration to CSR performance across a broad spectrum of values.

This is an open challenge to supply professionals to take a closer look at the introduction of chemicals and their responsible disposal.

A simple way to replace volatile organic compounds in cleaning products is to use a product that contains acetic acid a byproduct of bacteria called acetobacter. Commercial production uses cultured acetobacter for consistency. This alternative product is low cost and safe – commonly known as *white vinegar*!

Questions to Answer to Reduce Your Chemical Use

1. Do you have a comprehensive list of possible dangerous chemicals that your company uses or that your suppliers use?
2. Do you have a plan or policy for supply chain management to find ways to reduce chemical harm and find responsible disposal services?
3. Are you aware of the benchmarks that the Dow Jones Sustainability Indices (DJSI) uses for your industry?
4. Are you willing to link executive pay to important CSR accomplishments?
5. Do you know where choice editing would help reduce toxic chemicals?

#8 Focus: Green Office Products and Services

One of the lesser controversial areas to work in involving sustainability products is found in the office. Most retail and commercial office product companies have alternative products readily available. However not all green products are lower in cost. As a general rule the cost of office products is a low budget item in most organizations. If green products cost double on a few line items it would be hard to see an effect on the bottom line. A philosophical decision may need to be taken where the preference will be for green(er) products over cost.

Office products are a good way of building internal capacity for CSR. As I have said before, it is the low hanging fruit, like refillable non-toxic white board cleaners as a cost effective options. Increasing staff awareness on habits and services that they can control creates positive morale. Here are some good examples:

- Fax machines can easily be set up for electronic messages only.
- Laser fiche scanning is affordable and reduces mountains of paper over time with an expedient means of record retrieval.
- Paperless invoicing is affordable and efficient.
- Electronic fund transfer is not expensive and achieves business process improvements.
- Double-sided copying can be the default setting on printers with single-sided requiring a manual intervention each time.
- All waste papers should be collected and recycled.
- Vegetable-based inks should be used for business cards and other documents *where printing is necessary.*
- Refillable toner cartridges are low cost and require fewer resources to collect and reuse than buying new.
- Consider not handing out printed materials at meetings and conferences but provide e-copies only.
- Conference giveaway or swag bags should have biodegradable or recycled content materials.
- Vermicomposting (worm farm) can be set up in the office to process organic or food waste items. Remember Perkins+Will Canada's *Pass the Trash* competition?

Did you know that in 1990 *Xerox* designed their photocopiers to be able to be *deconstructed* for use in the new copiers today? This is an example of the Design for Environment (DFE) concept-reducing the use of resources, energy conservation and waste reduction to enable a sustainable supply. As well, the solid ink technology introduced by *Xerox* in 2009 is aimed at eliminating the concept of traditional ink cartridges.

Don't want to support big companies like *Xerox*? The introduction of managed print services is currently reengineering the copier and print business. Where traditional supply strategies lead to RFPs for paper, copiers printers and other consumables, managed print services provides organizational-wide solutions including records management. Managing agnostic brands under a single service provider was pioneered at the University of Calgary and subsequently followed by the University of British Columbia in 2009.

 ## Questions to Answer to Increase Green Office Products & Services

1. What internal office services can you get your organization on board to change to be more green?
2. How can you encourage the change in habits? (ex: Perkins+Will Canada's Pass the Trash competition).
3. What refillable or other green products can you start to buy or implement?
4. How can you eliminate the use of paper?

Moving Forward

Professional supply managers have a great deal of responsibility but also exciting challenges. Where sustainability factors such as reduced emissions or environmental standards are adopted compliance becomes an increasingly important decision criteria. Go slow, make small strides, celebrate successes until they become habits and then move on to the next solution. We have given you many things you can try on for size when starting to go green and implement CSR. A recap of all the questions you can ask your team is under our Resources.

The next stage after moving forward is to think about how you know if you are getting there: reporting.

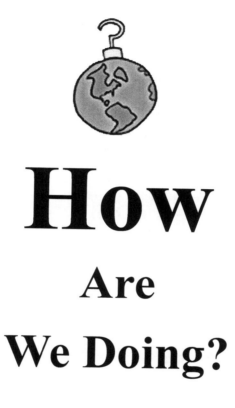

How

Are

We Doing?

How Are We Doing?

CSR Analysis Reporting

When it comes to creating reports on how you are doing, don't reinvent the wheel. For examples of the types of reporting metrics the Global Reporting Initiative (GRI) has many examples of reporting models based on a decade of experience. Their web site provides comprehensive information for various industries and market sectors including public agencies.

The GRI reports can be adapted by individual organizations to gain familiarity with reporting disciplines and compliance issues. This will require some investment in time and staffing resources to fully develop meaningful reports. Examples in supply management would come under the GRI category of Environmental Performance Indicators EN 1 through EN 30 for reports on related achievements including quantitative metrics. These indicators assess an organization's impact on the ecosystems. The report would require data on the types of materials and volumes consumed, recycled content, direct and indirect energy consumed, water sources, emissions effluents and waste, GHGs, supplier related activities to environmental programs, logistics, and expenditures in these areas.

At a minimum the GRI outline provides an excellent assessment tool for a company in terms of creating a more responsible business model. The company can self-audit to see where it aligns with GRI guidelines and where it needs to close the gaps. This is where the organization's leadership can decide to make a strategic philosophical change in direction or not. The comparative exercise could highlight advantages to commit to improving its social responses or environmental commitments enabling it to create a market differentiation strategy.

Tips for Reporting

- Work with your top ten suppliers along with the GRI metrics to share research and for mutual benefits.
- Reporting out is a strategic step and would be a long-term commitment and not a short-term project.
- Use metrics that measure human rights, health and safety, energy consumption, waste and resource conservation, emissions management, directed training programs, community projects, consumer protection and risk management relevant to these issues
- Also report on record supplier codes of conduct, any annual initiatives and targets for improvement corporate governance, any policy revisions and international standards of compliance with third party audits.
- Share your successes and celebrate them appropriately if possible
- Leading organizations have the common trait of publicly sharing their external reporting in addition to the traditional reports on profitability and mandatory accounting compliance.
- Leading organizations allow many other organizations to draw from this collective experience and adopt these objective-reporting tools for their needs.

Alongside GRI are the SA 8000, ISO 14001, and AA1000 Assurance Standard frameworks for reporting metrics. Although each has a specific focus they all intend to be transparent in content have adequate scope of operational technical administrative and corporate governance and enable organizations to be responsive to their respective stakeholders in a global sense.

Another remarkable business is the *B Lab* non-profit organization that has created the concept of the *B Corporation*—B meaning beneficial. Its purpose is to use business to address social and environmental problems. They have hundreds of large and small businesses as members in Canada and the US *Ethical Bean,* a leading coffee company, and *Mills Basics,* an office supply company, are socially responsible business advocates in Vancouver as members of *B Corp.*

To become a *B Corp* certified organization there is a rigorous set of criteria that must be followed and met. They use a set of 170 questions in an online survey to categorize its members. The comprehensive report distills down to a rating based on an organization's commitments on the environment, employees, community, consumers, and leadership. The resulting composite score gives the organization a sense of where it stands and where it can do better. Any organization vying for the *B Corp* certification must receive a minimum of 40 points out of 100.

Organizations that qualify to meet the *B Corp* rating must pay 1/10th of 1% of their revenues to *B Lab.* The claimed benefits of participating in the *B Corp* process lead to market differentiation and savings through a network of supplier organizations.

Whatever you decide to use in terms of reporting, don't underestimate its importance. Just as will all business goals and metrics, you can't know how well you are doing, whether against others or against last year, until you measure it.

Positive Corporate Benchmarks

In researching this book I met with hundreds of entrepreneurs who successfully incorporate CSR values into their business. Two, in particular, stand out that can be seen as benchmarks: *Protocol Environmental Solutions Inc.* and *Fairware*.

I was interested in what these two companies do that can be a model for other businesses and entrepreneurs undertaking CSR values on the sometimes perplexing road to sustainability. The CEOs of both these companies were passionate and their personal integrity showed in every aspect of what they do. CSR was not simply an attempt to be politically current, it was the very foundation of their corporate structure. I was also moved by how they are among a growing legion of entrepreneurs who are predisposed to look at long-term value, rather than simply short-term profit. Yet, they have not lost sight of the importance of profitability and the need to be cost conscious for their customers in order to remain competitive.

Both *Protocol* and *Fairware* successfully meet what I call the 3E's:
- Economic interests
- Environmental responsibilities
- And, societal Expectations

Protocol Environmental Solutions

Serial entrepreneur, Floyd Wandler, and his partner, Julia Raeder, founded *Protocol Environmental Solutions* in 2003. The name of their company says it all. They wanted to create environmental solutions that worked. They felt that far too many companies were ignoring green product opportunities because many early green products were costly and quite simply didn't work. So Floyd and Julia decided to develop new products that met the following three criteria:

- They must be as green as possible
- They must be cost effective
- And they must be effective in the real world—in other words they have to do what they claim.

"If you have all three of these elements you have a winner," said Floyd.

One key to their success was to make sure they created scalable solutions by contacting the biggest players in a particular market sector and discuss with them about the potential for a product solution. They didn't waste time on products where the margins were low, but focused on what is being done and what is not being done in the industry in general, as well as evaluating the potential size of the market.

The anti-fouling product for the marine industry is a good example of *Protocol* pro-actively solving a worldwide problem. Most marine vessels use copper coatings to protect the hull from salt water. These coatings are extremely toxic and difficult to both apply and remove. Small boat owners and huge tanker companies alike, need to regularly apply layers on top of existing coatings which leads to a problem of drag that requires more fuel simply to maintain speed. *Protocol* solved the problem by completely removing the anti-fouling coatings with a water-based biodegradable spray that can be applied and washed off within a few hours. The result was almost too good to be believed. The business advantage for *Protocol* is that there is no other product on the market capable of doing this.

"We look at the status quo in various industries and challenge what is accepted. We look for new ways to solve the problems. We are tenacious," said Floyd. "On the other hand you need to know when you have to cut the losses. No matter how good a product might work if people aren't buying it, move on. It may be a great product but the market may not be ready for it. We've morphed from graffiti removal to steam equipment to concrete treatments to mining, marine and oil and gas industry engineering applications. We are always looking for new ideas."

One of the first to come on board was *Overwaitea Foods. Protocol* redesigned *Overwaitea's* compactors and waste handling locations so they were much more efficient.

"We showed our customers how to make money from their garbage. We resized compactors and relocated them to where they should be. Our competition had the attitude that one-size-fits-all, which it doesn't. We exploited that flawed thinking."

What Protocol Does Right

Initially, *Protocol* thought they would be designing, producing and distributing their own product lines. However, they soon realized that their expertise was better suited to being a research and development company. They funded and built their own world-class laboratory where they research and develop products. This gives them a great advantage where they can continuously improve products to address the problems they are trying to solve for their customers. Through licensing and other venture options they choose to focus on new products and let others handle the downstream activities. *Protocol* sticks to what they do best.

One thing that *Protocol* decided early in their corporate stance was not to compete on price when it came to technologies. Instead they worked hand-in-hand with their customer for a solution that met their three criteria of being green, being cost effective and doing the job it's meant to do. They believe in doing their homework on a customer's problems and then developing a solution that meets the needs of all the parties.

Protocol developed a safe, heat tint remover that pickles and passivates stainless steel in a single step and contains no hydrofluoric acid. The use of hydrofluoric acid in traditional products is a chronic industry problem fraught with hazardous working conditions, costly to apply and costly to dispose of responsibly. *Praxair*, a global leader in industrial technologies, products and services was the first distribution company to value the benefits of eliminating hydrofluoric acid. Under its *ProStar®* label, *Praxair* now distributes this innovative technology from *Protocol*, offering its customers a sustainable and more responsible treatment solution. *Praxair's* mission is "making our planet more productive."

Protocol spends a lot of time listening to its customers. *Protocol's* proposed solutions require them to educate customers, as their recommendations may not be something they are familiar with. It is a very reciprocal process once they gain a customer's trust. Their customers want to share their ideas with *Protocol*, which is another way they find opportunities. Many sales groups overlook the problems that are right in front of them. *Protocol* shows how being a good listener is a wise business practice.

"We develop responsible products to solve customer problems that also help the planet. To be successful we have to be good at all facets of the business with sustainability being a core value," said Floyd.

Fairware

Denise Taschereau founded *Fairware* in 2005 out of a 400 square foot garage without any government grants. As an avid outdoors person and athlete, Denise had high respect for the environment. She believed that the simple act of buying was a very real way of changing the world. That is a bold statement, which she can now back up.

Creating *Fairware* was Denise's test to prove that CSR can also be good business. Her company continues to grow in the very competitive market of providing promotional merchandise for corporations. *Fairware* researches how every product they represent is made, where it is manufactured, how it is brought to market, and how it impacts peoples' lives across the supply chain. This constant research is the means to truly establishing their credibility in the market, and they spend a lot of time clarifying these issues for their clients to help them make informed decisions.

"We have clients that may be using a vinyl product that is not an environmentally friendly material but is cheap. We make suggestions to provide better alternatives. We get them to stop and think about their choices," says Denise.

Fairware's Values

Fairware's success is founded on three beliefs in looking at their own company and their suppliers:

1. The Mud of the company
2. The Morals of the company
3. The Management of the company

The mud is the risk-based perspective of looking at a particular brand's supply chain issues as well as their social and environmental decisions.

Morals are addressed through a mission-based philosophy that keeps *Fairware* on track to make a difference. And management practices focus on efficiencies, compliance, performance and culture. "We're not about the stuff, we're how to drive change with the stuff," explains Denise. This is how *Fairware* builds trust and relationship with their customers.

In addition, they use a survey developed by McMaster University and ask all their vendors the following questions:
- Where are their head offices?
- What countries they are supplying from?
- Do they have a code of conduct?
- What types of remediation processes do they have in place?
- Do they have any certification on their facilities?
- Do they have any audit reports?

From there, they cross-reference the survey with other third party audit organizations and pay for third party reports when required. They also interview their supplier's social compliance directors. "We do our homework because that is our currency. Most clients don't want the details – they trust us to verify and check all references through a process of due diligence. Clients trust our recommendations," Denise concludes.

Corporate culture is also very important to *Fairware*. Through a variety of activities including: Ride-a-kid's-bike-to-work event, brain storming field trips, flexible hours, a monthly Salad Club, Sundaes-on-Mondays and Fun Fridays they have successfully created a fun work environment. Every morning at 10:00am *Fairware* holds "ten-ten" meetings to be sure everyone knows and can support the other team members' projects. The attention to culture is an integral part of their business strategy.

Lessons from the Benchmarks

There are many parallels between the partners of *Protocol* and *Fairware*. Both are among a growing legion of entrepreneurs who base their entire business model on being sustainable. They attract customers who are eager to be more responsible in their purchasing choices and educate them in how those decisions make a difference. They are profit-driven, but with a conscious effort to do so by mitigating the inevitable consequences to the environment. And, they acknowledge there aren't always perfect decisions. Being on the leading edge, they are aware that they must keep abreast of innovations in technology as well as being socially responsible for the impact all industry has on society and the natural world.

Both *Protocol* and *Fairware* successfully demonstrate that:
- CSR is a viable way of conducting business
- Being competitive need not strictly be price-based
- Differentiating from the competition is a matter of leading, not following
- Success comes from targeting discerning customers
- Relationships are long-term and built through trust
- The supply chain is a conduit to facilitate change
- Innovation creates value

Entrepreneurs like *Protocol* and *Fairware*, while pursuing completely different market sectors, are raising the bar for others to follow. They show that in the right hands business can make a positive difference.

Their customers too share similar values and choose to purchase from companies who demonstrate an alignment with their corporate philosophies.

While we must continue to draw on the forests, oceans, rivers, minerals, and fossil fuels for many more generations, I believe it is through innovative thinkers and the businesses they create that we will make the crucial shift towards the care and well-being of our planet. After all, it's the only one we have.

Design for Environment

A great deal of our production thinking has been based narrowly on maximizing efficiencies and designing for ease of manufacturing and shipping. Many consumer, commercial and industrial goods have been designed for disposal as opposed to taking the Design for Environment (DFE) approach. Landfill sites were the previous solution to disposal. Low cost resources made it cheaper to extract new raw materials rather than design products that used fewer resources. Spewing fumes into the air was a lower cost than trying to reduce CO_2 emissions. Cheap oil allowed for building designs that wasted energy on a 24/7 basis and they still do. If companies want to move from red faces to facing the world with good news they need to incorporate DFE in everything they do, including redesigning and refitting their wasteful designs. CSR Consultants and third-party audit companies can help any company that sincerely wants to adopt DFE practices get started. If you wish to learn about a host of Vancouver companies using biomimicry and DFE in creative ways, see the latest book by Lea Elliott, *Nature Rules* (*naturehood.ca*).

Greenwashing and Red Faces

(What NOT to do)

Greenwashing organizations are known as 'stuffed olives'
—they are green on the outside and red on the inside.
- Larry Berglund

Just as critical to what you do now and will do is what you should not do. If you are in a rush to "look good" by doing the right thing, you may not be doing the right thing at all.

Greenwashing

Labeling a product or service is used to influence customers' decisions, and it works. It works so well that the marketing industry of labeling and using word spin is thriving and consumers are buying whatever the latest trends are: non-GMO, Gluten-Free, All Natural, Organic, etc. Exaggerated benefits do a disservice to the credibility of the green movement and sustainability in general. It also speaks to the problems of labeling in Canada and the corporate ethical behavior of the companies behind the claims.

In 2007, *TerraChoice Environmental Marketing Inc.*, published an article on the *Six Sins of Greenwashing*™ and reviewed the labels of 1000+ products from air fresheners to writing instruments that claimed that they were green. Of 1700 environmental claims, all but one was false or misleading.

179

TerraChoice have now added a 7th sin and have created a website: http://sinsofgreenwashing.org/ that even has a game, called, Name That Sin.

The Sins of Greenwashing were as follows:

1. **Hidden trade-offs**—essentially suggesting that something small in process is greener or a green practice all by itself
2. **No proof**
3. **Vagueness**
4. **Irrelevance**—truthful claim that goes on the public's ignorance of what is actually green
5. **Lying**
6. **Lesser of two evils**—distracting consumer from greater environmental evils
7. **Worshiping false labels**—a suggestion of third party endorsement that does **not exist.**

I am going to add an 8th sin of greenwashing:

8. **Managerial Buzzwords of Commitment**—when management creates their own spin words of commitment to CSR and does not walk the talk

Many organizations will draft and publicize their policy commitments towards protecting the environment or community involvement and place them visibly throughout the organization or in its publications. However, when push comes to shove, few will stand by and forego profit over self-serving short–term interests. Or, they will not bring the role of sustainability into job descriptions. Some believe adding it to job descriptions may invite pay increases which will become precedent setting, which is not necessarily true. They will also not support short-term price increases to introduce green alternative products if they think there won't be fast paybacks. Often these decisions within the organization are made arbitrarily and based on one individual's definition of value.

Greenwashing can also occur on the part of the supply chain professional buying for an organization. The buyer may imply to their suppliers that they want to purchase greener goods and services yet will award a contract for traditional products for marginal savings. Suppliers are confused by these mixed signals. Where organizations have adopted progressive sustainability sourcing policies they must also support those statements in their actions. Certainly the impact on the bottom line must be assessed, but the longer-term benefits must be concurrently weighed.

The *Canadian Competition Bureau* announced their guidelines for green products published as: *Environmental Claims: A Guide for Industry and Advertisers* (http://www.bureaudelaconcurrence.gc.ca >Publications Technical Guidance Documents> Enforcement Guidelines) to clarify the acceptable terminology when marketing green products. The American version of this is the FTC's Green Guides (https://www.ftc.gov >News & Events> Media Resources> Truth In Advertising> Green Guides)

Although these guides are helpful for consumers and marketers, it could have more relevance and benefit to the clean technology sector, which is bringing new technology products to market. There is a one-year transition period to allow businesses to adapt to the new guidelines.

Unfortunately, questionable labeling practices will likely continue to skew the information in favor of the seller. Companies that see CSR policy as an *end* to sell green customers and not as a *means* to produce something that meets their requirements are likely the same ones that commit one or more of the *TerraChoice's* seven greenwashing sins. Making sure you are not committing the 8th sin and you will likely not commit the others.

Red Faces—More Examples Not To Follow

At the heart of sustainability for business leaders is the realization that resources such as water and air have been grossly undervalued. The pollution of these resources as a result of business operations has largely been externalized – meaning society has paid most of the costs.

The true cost of producing and consuming energy has not been fully loaded. It is affecting all of the below and will continue to get worse in all these areas:

- Unsustainable economics with many goods increasing in expense
- Undermining and exploiting the developing world
- Dangerously elevated CO_2 levels that contribute to catastrophic climate changes
- Undervaluing resources making food production unsustainable
- Extirpation or extinction of species

If we concede that we have undervalued natural resources such as air, soil, and water we must consider that we have undervalued plants and wild life. This has led to the situation of irreversibility – the extinction of a species. Extinction may be localized or global but once gone they often take out a critical part of the micro and macro eco systems which threatens hundreds and thousands of other species. Current rate according a recent Duke University study: 100 extinctions per million species per year, or **1,000 times** higher than natural rates. They also predict that future rates may be as much as **10,000 times** higher. The work of the *International Union for Conservation of Nature* (IUCN) is to link biodiversity to the well-being of people.

Biodiversity is important to business. The loss of natural resources and habitats leads to the cumulative degradation of our environment and quality of life. If fishing practices continue to dredge the sea bottom or clear cut logging practices go unchecked or the use of toxic materials is allowed or the dumping of waste into landfills and oceans is permitted or the draining of wetlands for warehouses, we will continue the depletion of resources and extinction of species on the planet. Simple equation is: no planet – no business!

What needs to become extinct are the gas and oil industry in favor of renewable green energy resources. However, it is not just energy companies that we can blame. Any company who is not first and foremost working on reducing their emissions and dependence on oil and gas are culpable. Newsweek and other publications often report the worst offenders for their environmental apathy and harmful practice, however it is rare for any company to be taking their energy reduction seriously or looking at alternative sources of energy, for sustainability reasons.

Disclosure Problem

Here are some big companies that could do better given their profits, and are hard to pin down since they are far from giving full disclosure to the public:

• *Visa*	• *MasterCard*	• *Nike*
• *Amazon*	• *Facebook*	• *Prada*
• *KFC*	• *MacDonald's*	• *Avon*
• *Harley Davidson*	• *Ralph Lauren*	• Many others can do better

Ref: https://www.future500.org/top-global-brands-best-worst-sustainability-disclosures/, 2014
Choosing only the brands that are not recognized by the EPA on their current website: http://www.epa.gov/greenpower/toplists/fortune500.htm

These are the tip of the iceberg. They are listed mostly because their record of disclosure in proportion to their economic success alone is shameful. If they did have disclosure and had decent CSR practices, they could be world leaders and have something better than profits to talk about. The problem is, they have already dominated their competition but they mostly have traditional mindsets.

But, what about SMEs that we mentioned before? Smaller, private companies can make an enormous difference.

Here are some segments of smaller private companies that need to start trying:

- Virtually all private finance companies
- Many of the mining companies
- Many ski resort companies for their water usage (to make snow)
- Many retail clothing companies

The problem with privately held companies is we often have even less information than publically held companies. Yet, as mentioned before, they make up much of the economy and can make the largest differences. Those smaller companies who are doing their CSR, need to start crowing about their CSR successes and make their competition and the public stand up and take notice.

Other Red Face Practices

There are a range of other practices that should infuriate us and motivate us to force change as well as be doubly sure that our own companies are not supporting suppliers in the following ways:

- Exploitive practices using child and forced labor has enabled corporate profits in an often criminal manner.

- Using waterways as an "industrial toilet" allowed organizations to avoid responsibility for processing costs.
- Selling electronic waste to offshore brokers was an easy way to rid us of obsolete electronics while producing another environmental nightmare elsewhere.
- Beaching oil tankers in India to have them cut into scrap by hundreds of laborers was a cost saving strategy with great negative social and environmental outcomes.
- Politicizing the use of corn for fuel so it panders to one group of constituents at the expense of the greater interests of society.
- Deregulation of financial markets allowed self-serving interests to exceed society's interests

The last point on deregulation of the markets is another red face for our politicians, for the financial industry and also for all of us, the public, for letting them get away with it. Fortunately, the legions of innovators, capital conscientious investors, progressive legislators, and concerned consumers are bringing many new sustainable products and services to the market. This is our great hope that business will find the equilibrium between economic interests and environmental responsibility to meet the evolving expectations of societies. It is the sense of urgency that needs to be applied with the will to problem solve rather than deferring the decision until one's shift is over.

Conclusion

I would like to see everybody spend a little bit of time thinking about the consequences of the little choices they make every day—what we buy, what we eat, what we wear.
~ *Jane Goodall*

I'm often asked what the biggest impediment is to implementing more responsible business strategies. It is not a lack of policies. It is not a lack of best practices. It is not a lack of strategic knowledge. It is not a lack of expertise. It is not a lack of funds. It is a lack of professional fortitude to leverage the resources at hand to do more social and economic good because it invites a level of personal risk. Some of the benefits may not appear on your shift. The fear of failure or criticism outweighs the potential to demonstrate value by exercising one's personal and professional integrity. At a minimum, point out to other decision makers where the choices can be made; and wherever possible, choose to make a difference in affecting social and economic values within a business case.

The movement to adopt a circular economy, built around the idea of eliminating waste, recognizes the opportunities across the supply chain to conserve resources and sustain profitability. Getting it right at the design stage to recover materials for future purposes acknowledges our reliance on finite resources. For the past 200+ years we built an economy around the consumption of infinite resources and today we find the cupboard is bare. But it can be refilled.

The circular economy movement envisioned by Ellen MacArthur (https://www.ellenmacarthurfoundation.org), will require supply chains to rethink their role. Reverse logistics and deconstructable products will drive the changes. Major European companies are taking the circular economy seriously.

Resources and research are being applied to technologies and in business models that can compete and contribute to creating value. The definition of value includes all three factors: profits, people, and the planet. We are fortunate to see individuals and businesses demonstrating that a balance can be struck within the framework of conscious capitalism. Adapting leading practices becomes easier as exemplary organizations share their views and provide the kind of leadership that affects market sectors and continues to spread CSR as a ripple around the globe.

The worst case scenario is that we find another planet in a solar system that we could afford to colonize. This would take the focus off our existing sustainability issues on the Earth and literally turn it into a waste dump. Space travel would be for those that could afford it and leave behind about 99% of the people that couldn't. With tongue in cheek, marketing experts and spin doctors would give it a name like Nuevo Planeta Azul (New Blue Planet) to develop the terrestrial real estate. The financial community using loosely regulated derivatives would ensure low risk to the first groups of investors with an expectation that real estate prices could only increase. The remaining taxpayers on Earth would understandably bailout any failures as these types of investments would be too big to allow them to fail.

With attention on our Nuevo Planeta Azul research and resources would be devoted entirely to that project. Unfortunately given the history of the occupancy of people on planet Earth, Nuevo Planeta Azul's population of 60 million would also be exploited within 250 years – the length of time we have been industrialized to date with acceleration due to our learning curve on consumptive practices. Nuevo Planeta Azul would soon resemble our Earth today with similar problems of sustainability.

The textbooks and courses for business are being written now with new chapters on sustainability and corporate social responsibility. The ink is still wet and new experiences are being gained and included each day. Do your homework and it will pay off. Whether you believe in global warming or climate change does not matter. If you agree that lower costs, lower emissions, healthier communities, better value propositions, resource conservation, and cleaner air and water can result from changing the status quo, then start making those changes that are within your current capabilities. To look out to the future, expand your mandate to be more inclusive in a strategic approach and provide the leadership organizations and society are in need of. We will eventually get it right because we have to!

The ability to affect change is not without risks. Inaction invites greater risks. The information in this book is intended to provide you with guidance on why, where, how you can take responsibility for your actions. Business is the cause of many of the problems while it is also the catalyst for the solutions. For too long we have ensured profits based on a narrow number of stakeholders deriving most of the benefits. We need to balance the profits with the planet and the people. We have the talent and resources to do this. Now exercise the leadership fortitude to enact conscious capitalism in practice. If we acknowledge the responsibility to accept our share of the effort to make a difference, we can profit and progress in a sustainable model.

Good planets are hard to buy. What will you do for your planet tomorrow?

Appendix

Reminder of Risks of Not Doing CSR

1. Allowing our **Competition to get Market Share Through Better Corporate Image and Brand Reputation** from CSR approval
2. Allowing there to be an **Uneven Playing Field for International Business that Can Hurt Our Business**
3. Allowing an **Inefficient Use of Resources** that wastes money and a future business model
4. Allowing a **Reduction and Depletion (and Extinction) of Necessary Natural Resources**
5. Allowing the **Best Employees to be Attracted and Retained by Our Competition that have CSR Standards.**
6. Allowing our **Costs to Rise with Dependence on Oil-Based Products**
7. Allowing **Our Competition to Get Ahead on Reducing Operating Costs (&/or Increasing Profits)**
8. Allowing an **Imbalance of Social Wealth to Social Well-being**
9. Allowing **Our Competition to Increase Customer Sales and Loyalty**

Recap of All What to Do First Questions:

1. Have you figured out your GHG sources (Sources 1-3) to analyze your reduction strategy?

2. Can you be ahead of the game (regulations or taxes to come) and agree to lead the industry?

3. Have you looked at realistic offsetting and ways to implement it creatively?

4. Can you create a competitive challenge to help get the word out to your employees and suppliers?

5. Have you contacted organization that can give you expert help whether is be implementing ISO or using third party service providers like *Offsetters?*

6. How are you going to help control packaging from your company or your suppliers?

7. What other ways can packaging be reduced or replaced with biodegradable packaging?

8. What resources will you use to ensure alternative packaging truly is sustainable and biodegradable?

9. Are you in an industry where local sourcing makes sense both economically and for sustainability?

10. With each procurement, do you have a way to analyze which has more CSR value: local sourcing or another sourcing? Are your policies written to allow for this?

11. Are there ways for you to leverage local alternative energy sources and local transportation opportunities?

12. Can you lead the industry by creating a local efficiency model?

13. Do you have a sustainable employee travel policy and programs?

14. Have you investigated offsetting?

15. Have you analyzed and created a teleconferencing and a telecommuting policy and program in your organization?

16. Have you looked into your supplier for courier and cartage services to see if they are operating at a higher sustainability level

17. Can your own product sales and services choice edit for your buyers?

18. Do the retailers you support also support conscious choice editing for a better planet?

19. Have you done an analysis of the possible benefits of retrofitting your building?

20. Have you looked for consultants or organizations that can help you in a retrofit analysis or project?

21. Do you have a comprehensive list of possible dangerous chemicals that your company uses or Do you have a plan or policy for supply chain management to find ways to reduce chemical harm and find responsible disposal services?

22. Do you have a plan or policy for supply chain management to find ways to reduce chemical harm and find responsible disposal services?

23. Are you aware of the benchmarks that the Dow Jones Sustainability Indices (DJSI) uses for your industry?

24. Are you willing to link executive pay to important CSR accomplishments?

25. What internal office services can you get your organization on board to change?

26. How can you encourage the change in habits? (ex: Busby Perkins+Will Canada's *Pass the Trash* competition).

27. What refillable or other green products and services can you start to buy or implement?

Glossary of Acronyms and Terms

3Es	Economic interests, Environmental responsibilities, Expectations of Society
3Ps	People, Profits and the Planet
Clean Tech.	Clean technology includes recycling, renewable energy, information technology, green transportation, electric motors, green chemistry, lighting, energy efficient appliances, building products, and can include environmental finance (finance based on carbon credits). It is a means to create technology products and services that specifically are designed to minimize or eliminate negative environmental impacts.
CSR	Corporate Social Responsibility
CAMSC	Canadian Aboriginal & Minority Supplier Council
CFC	Chlorofluorocarbons as a volatile derivative of methane, ethane, and propane. They are also commonly known by the DuPont brand name Freon and contribute to the depletion of the ozone layer and acceleration of climate change.
DFE	Design for Environment
EPP	Ethical Procurement Policy
ESG	Environmental Social and Governance
FT	Fair Trade
GHG	Green House Gas

HCFC	Hydrochlorinated fluorocarbon is a fluorocarbon that is replacing chlorofluorocarbon as a refrigerant and propellant in aerosol cans and considered to be somewhat less destructive to the atmosphere (but still destructive)
HVAC	Heating Ventilation Air Conditioning
ILO	International Labour Organization
INGO	International Non Governmental Organization
ISO	International Standards Organization
LCA	Life Cycle Assessment
LCC	Life Cycle Costing
LEED	Leadership in Energy and Environmental Design
MNC	Multi National Corporation
MOR	Maintenance, Operating and Repair
MSN	Maquila Solidarity Network is a labor and women's rights organization that supports the efforts of workers in global supply chains to win improved wages and working conditions
NFP	Not For Profit
NGO	Non Governmental Organizations
OECD	Organization for Economic Co-Operation & Development
PESTEL	Political Environmental Social Technical Economic Legal
PLA	Polylactic Acid is a biodegradable thermoplastic aliphatic polyester derived from renewable resources
PVC	Polyvinyl Chloride is the third-most widely produced polymer, and has several toxic elements to it.
RFP	Request for Proposal
SAWP	Seasonal Agricultural Worker Program

SCM   Supply Chain Management includes: Buyers, Purchasers, Analysts, Coordinators, Managers and other professional roles in Supply Chain areas.

SCMA   Supply Chain Management Association

SCMP   Supply Chain Management Professional

SE   Social Enterprise

SME   Small Medium Enterprise

SWOT   Strengths Weaknesses Opportunities Threats

TCO   Total Cost of Ownership
         TCO is a financial estimate intended to help buyers and owners determine the direct and indirect **costs** of a product or system. It is a management accounting concept that can be used in full **cost** accounting or even ecological economics where it includes social **costs**.

VABE   Values Assumptions Beliefs Expectations

VOC   Volatile Organic Compound

WCI   Western Climate Initiative

WHMIS   Workplace Hazardous Material Information System

Resources

- TransFair USA
- Electronic Product Environmental Assessment Tool (EPEAT™)
- Energy Star®
- Green Seal™
- The Forest Stewardship Council (FSC)
- Verité
- International Organization for Standardization (ISO)
- Leadership in Energy and Environmental Design (LEED®)
- Marine Stewardship Council
- Restriction of Hazardous Substances (RoHS)
- Social Accountability 8000 (SA 8000)
- The Worker Rights Consortium (WRC)
- Fair Labor Association (FLA)
- Ecologic labels
- Waste Electrical and Electronic Equipment Directive (WEEE)
- Worldwide Responsible Apparel Production (WRAP©)

A comprehensive listing of eco-labels can be found at the Greener Choices website www.greenerchoices.org which is updated by Consumer Reports©. For other resources go to: www.LarryBerglund.com

Index

A

B

G

H

I

J

K

L

M

R

S

Endnotes

[1]   *Slippery Slopes and Misconduct: The Effect of Gradual Degradation on the Failure to Notice Others' Unethical Behavior*, HBS Working Paper #06-007, Francesca Gino and Max Bazerman. Graduate School of Business Administration, Harvard University, Revised February 18, 2007

[2]   *Going Paperless: Here's How it's Done...* by Basil Waugh in *UBC Reports,* volume 54, University of British Columbia, February 7th, 2008

[3]   Stats regarding SMEs: Canada: http://www.ic.gc.ca/eic/site/061.nsf/eng/02806.html. USA: http://www.sbecouncil.org/about-us/facts-and-data/

About the Author

Larry Berglund | SCMP | MBA | FSCMA

Larry Berglund draws experience from five decades of supply chain management leadership in the forest industry, public health care, municipal government, university operations, and consulting for a variety of other industries. He received his MBA degree from Athabasca University and worked with several other prestigious universities and organizations. His white paper on "Sustainable Supply Chain Management Practices" won first prize in the practitioner category at McMaster University.

He teaches supply chain management courses, webinars, and workshops and has written many articles in this area of expertise. As well, he has published *Better Ways to Better Deals: The Buyer/Seller Negotiation Handbook,* and *Food, Finance, and Philosophy: A Role for Supply Management in Corporate Social Responsibility.* He consults for a variety of organizations and presents training programs to sales organizations and buyers in both Canada and the U.S.

To share your opinions or ideas on sustainability and CSR please contact Larry at: LarryBerglund.com. or e-mail him at lberglund@prezplus.com.

62692435R00118

Made in the USA
Lexington, KY
15 April 2017